The Narrow Way Teachings

Straight from the Mouth of Jesus

Ke Russo

For every person who wants to follow Jesus without compromise. May you hear Jesus in this book. May faith, not fear, be the defining mark of your walk.

Acknowledgments

There are many who have covered this effort in their prayers. They have given me encouragement and constructive criticism. Others have given their time and energy in their busy lives to read this book in advance. My family has been understanding of demands that have required my time with this effort instead of being with them. For these special people, I am grateful. You would not be reading this book without them.

I am especially grateful for God touching my heart to delve into these teachings of Jesus. He planted the seed decades ago through a beloved professor. Through the years he watered that seed by drawing me into committing these teachings to heart. Like the prophet Jeremiah, these teachings became a fire in my bones that had to come out somehow. You now hold that *somehow*.

I am thankful to you for having the desire to read this book, and having the willingness to allow Jesus to teach you through me. I am most humbled by it all.

Endorsements

This book is for anyone who is Jesus-curious, who has heard about Jesus but is bewildered about how to start following him. Ke Russo is a minister who cares about Jesus and the people trying to follow Jesus. He is a gentle soul with long experience meeting people just outside and helping them to find a way in, to start following Jesus on a pathway toward a more meaningful life, a pathway toward God.

Christopher R. Hutson, PhD
Professor of Bible, Missions & Ministry
Associate Dean, College of Biblical Studies

***

The Narrow Way Teachings has a profound way of pointing the reader in the right direction. It encourages hearts and minds to embrace the teachings given solely from Jesus. The author carefully exegeted five blocks of teachings giving every reader the awareness needed to know who or what they are really following.

I can personally say as I read through these teachings, I couldn't help but mirror myself with the life of Christ. In doing this, I was forced to examine my journey as a disciple. I revisited seasons where I was more a disciple of persuasive preachers and religious fads than being one for Jesus. So open your heart to receive the wisdom needed to become a true disciple for Jesus. Throughout this dynamic study of the Word, you will truly see that the narrow way is the way that leads to life.

Author Shelia Pearson

***

God brought Ke Russo and I together at a time when my family and I were in a ministry to help with the basic needs of migrants who arrived from different parts of Central America to Matamoros, Mexico. After that occasion, I invited him to teach a course on the gospel of Matthew in our School of Preaching. On both occasions, I saw a compassionate man with great passion for empowering Our Lord's disciples with the knowledge of Christ's teachings.

I find <u>The Narrow Way Teachings: Straight from the Mouth of Jesus</u> to be a very useful book where we are challenged to analyze, adjust and correct our lives as disciples of Christ. Comparing them with teachings that Christ left regarding the way of life for His true disciples, and thus, verify if we are indeed on the right path.

José Cabello
Servant at Palmview Church of Christ and South Texas School of Preaching

***

This book is one of the most in depth looks at what being a disciple of Jesus Christ really is and what it isn't. If you are a person struggling to wrap your mind around Jesus, His teachings and just knowing Him overall this is a great book that will help you rewire your brain from all of the misconceptions and misinformation relating to this topic. I highly recommend this book because it is an overall self check for all people. Absolutely love this!

Summer M. Davis, Gen Z

***

This work is sensitive, relevant, and timely on the matter of living in the will of God. Ke Russo skillfully puts forth the need for people to return to God. It is a book I shall gladly recommend in any company.

RC Rayborn, Jr New Life Church

***

The narrow way teachings are so needed for such a time as this. Just when we thought the world could not get more divided, politically and religiously, we have the greatest divide ever. This exposé, five sections of the book of Matthew brings us together by carefully understanding the simple teachings of Jesus that breaks down walls, exposes the love of God, brings the powerful light of truth and brings a life of unity to all who will embrace the narrow way teachings of Jesus.

Elder Leonardo Gilbert, minister Sheldon Heights Church of Christ

Contents

Introduction

Picture in your mind a sailing ship with tall masts, sailing the seas in the early 1800s. Visualize the ship being tossed up and down, back and forth, by angry waves; each wave sweeps over the deck, threatening to wash every sailor overboard. The skies are dark, lit up only by the bolts of lightning streaking across the sky. Strong winds hammer the boat and its sailors with stinging rain. The captain is at the helm, doing little more than preventing the ship from being broadsided by the next angry wave. Everyone else is just holding tight, trying to ride out the storm. The hours drag by, and the storm is unrelenting. Slowly, the winds die down, and the waves cease. Almost magically, the storm is replaced by peaceful calm and smooth seas. Gradually, the stars begin to reappear in the sky. Everyone breathes easier now, for the storm is past. But where are they? No one knows, yet no one worries. The captain and the sailors will find their bearings and resume their journey across the ocean.

Perhaps you have wondered how sailors can find their way across a vast ocean without getting lost. I guarantee you that you do not want me as the captain of your ship on an ocean voyage. My problem would not be getting lost; my problem would be that I would start out lost and not know how to get unlost. Yet knowledgeable sailors have no problem with getting lost on the ocean. If they have the North Star and a timepiece called a chronometer, they will always know where they are and which direction to sail.

How is that possible? The North Star and the chronometer help them know two very important bits of information — latitude and longitude.

If they know those two things, they can pinpoint their location on a map and know which way to sail in order to get to their destination. For our purposes, we are just focusing on how sailors use the North Star to find their latitude and find their way.

Navigating the ocean requires finding and following the North Star, which remains a constant point of reference in the night sky. While I struggle to identify it, experienced sailors do not, and they rely on this steadfast guide. They understand how to follow a star that does not move, and that is key. The North Star does not move in the night sky because it sits directly above true north. So a captain needs only to find the North Star to know what direction north is. If north is the desired direction, the captain just keeps the ship going in that direction. If the direction is somewhere west, the captain just points the ship in a direction west of the star. That is how a captain knows which direction to go.

How does the captain find the latitude of the ship's location using the North Star? Incredibly, noting how high the North Star is in the sky tells the captain the exact latitude of the ship on the earth. The number of degrees the North Star is from the horizon from the ship's perspective happens to be the number of degrees the ship is from the equator. That gives the captain that key bit of information. How does the captain find the number of degrees the North Star is from the horizon? Well, he (or she) can extend his (or her) arms, make two fists, and stack them on top of each other from the horizon to the location of the North Star. Each fist represents roughly ten degrees. If three fists are needed to mark the distance between the horizon and the North Star, that is roughly thirty degrees. The captain need only find the thirty-degree latitude line on a map after that. If the ship captain wants a more precise way to find the exact degrees, he or she would use a sextant, which measures the exact degrees. A similar principle, with a slight twist, is used with the sun to find latitude in the daytime. Once the captain knows the latitude of the ship's location, he or she is halfway home to finding the ship's exact location on the ocean.

In the image that you visualized in your mind, a ship sitting in calm seas after a storm, it was only a matter of time before the captain would determine their current location so they could continue their journey. They were never lost because they had the information needed to get back on course.

No one likes getting lost, even less so staying lost. This is true in any aspect of life. It is especially true with the spiritual journeys we take as well. So how do we travel the stormy seas of life without getting lost spiritually? Just like God gave sailors the North Star for sailing the seas, He has given all people a spiritual North Star: Jesus. We need only know how to find Him and then follow Him to keep from getting lost.

You may ask: *Why is Jesus the North Star?* You may ask that question because you do not lean toward a Christian persuasion. You could be a member of some other world religion like Judaism, Islam, Buddhism, Hinduism, Sikhism... There are plenty to choose from, and people all over the world are doing so. You may even consider yourself to be an agnostic or an atheist. In this world, there are a considerable number of people who do not see a need to follow some historical person called Jesus.

If that is where you are, let me give you a brief and quick overview of why Jesus is that North Star. In the Christian Bible, two books inform us that Jesus was born in Bethlehem at a certain time (Matthew and Luke). In another gospel, Jesus claims that a full life is experienced only through Him (John 10:10). He also claims to be the Son of God (John 1:14), to be the only way to His Father (John 14:6), to be the source of truth (John 8:31), and to be the ultimate truth (John 14:6). In Acts 2:22-36 and in Philippians 2:6-11, it is taught that Jesus was killed, buried, and raised from the dead. The claim of the resurrection is the foundation for claiming Jesus is the King and judge of all people. That makes Jesus our God-given spiritual North Star if all of these claims are true.

Are they true? There are ancient historical records that verify that Jesus actually did live in Israel from 4 B.C. to 29 A.D. They verify that He was indeed crucified by Pontius Pilate. The historicity of Jesus is not denied. What is questioned is His claim to divinity. In that regard, there is an interesting event at Jesus' crucifixion that was validated by an ancient historian who did not accept that Jesus was the Son of God. His name was Thallus, and he wrote his historical records around 50 A.D., just eleven years after Jesus was crucified. There was an occurrence of darkness during Jesus' crucifixion that lasted for hours. Thallus wrote that the darkness was the result of a solar eclipse. Later, another writer, Julius Africanus, wrote that a solar eclipse was not possible because the Passover was held during the time of a full moon, thus making a solar eclipse impossible because the moon was in the wrong place for such an eclipse. So Thallus, in attempting to discredit the miraculous stories surrounding Jesus' death, actually validated one of those miracles.

The linchpin to Jesus' claim of being the Son of God, though, is whether or not He was raised from the dead as was claimed by His disciples. Fifty days after Jesus was crucified, His disciples preached in Jerusalem that Jesus was no longer dead, that He was risen from the dead, and that the resurrection was God's proof that Jesus is the Son of God and the King of all people. The very Sanhedrin Council of the Jews and the Roman Army that had killed Jesus were still there in Jerusalem. They knew about the preaching of those disciples of Jesus at the temple that day. They were still enemies of Jesus. If Jesus' dead body had been produced by His executioners, the proclaimed resurrection would have been easily disproved. The Roman soldiers guarding the grave could have simply presented His dead body to the public, ending the movement before it ever started. Those disciples would have been revealed to be lying and they would have been disregarded by the people. It would have been that simple.

Stopping the movement of Jesus' followers was in Rome's best interest. Caesar wanted no rival kings to arise and bring unrest and revolt to his empire. Earlier Caesars had killed others who claimed to be such a king for the Jews. The Roman soldiers would have had no qualms about bringing out a dead body and showing it to the people, but they did not. That means we can know that Jesus was indeed risen from the dead, and He is indeed the Son of God.

There is more proof for us that Jesus is our spiritual North Star. We have twenty-seven books of the Christian Bible that would have never been written if Jesus' dead body had been produced that day by the Roman soldiers. When you thumb through a Bible with a New Testament or see numerous Bibles on a shelf in a bookstore or library, you are looking at evidence. That means Jesus did all the miracles in those twenty-seven books. That means all His bold claims about His identity are true, and you will find yourself one day standing before Him, with Him as your judge. That makes Jesus the spiritual North Star everybody needs to follow.

So how does one actually follow Jesus? What does that look like? Does it mean becoming a member of some Christian denomination, attending church services every Sunday, or at least on Christian holidays? Following Jesus can mean any number of things to people, and over the centuries, it has. To get us all on the same wavelength, I offer this picture: following Jesus is about traveling down a road.

In 1915, Robert Frost wrote a poem entitled The Road Not Taken:

Two roads diverged in a yellow wood,
And sorry I could not travel both
And be one traveler, long I stood
And looked down one as far as I could
To where it bent in the undergrowth;

Then took the other, as just as fair,
And having perhaps the better claim,
Because it was grassy and wanted wear;
Though as for that the passing there
Had worn them really about the same,

And both that morning equally lay

In leaves no step had trodden black.

Oh, I kept the first for another day!

Yet knowing how way leads on to way,

I doubted if I should ever come back.

I shall be telling this with a sigh

Somewhere ages and ages hence:

Two roads diverged in a wood, and I—

I took the one less traveled by,

And that has made all the difference.

The powerful words of this poem stir the imagination and paint vivid pictures in one's mind. It speaks to the reality that every life chooses to travel down a road that leads somewhere. We make conscious decisions to travel those roads. The road may be a career choice. It could be the decision to marry or not marry, to have children or not have children. It could be a decision on where to live. Maybe sometimes we look back and wonder what our lives would have been like if we had chosen the other road. In essence, life is a series of journeys down a number of roads that a person chooses to travel.

Jesus brings us to another road that we can choose or not choose. This choice is made while walking down our other roads of life. However, when we come to this choice about following Jesus, the fork presents two roads that create seismic shifts that ripple into every crevice of one's life. One road is the choice not to follow Jesus; the other road is the choice to follow Him. We can see a slight distance down each road, but mostly the roads have unknown twists and turns, hills, and valleys. It is not possible to know what the chosen road is really like until it is traveled and experienced. We discover then if we made the right choice. Standing at the fork, one thing is clear: the road less traveled is the one that follows Jesus. This can be both scary and exciting. The possibility of wonder and adventure draws us; the possibility of loneliness and even opposition pushes us toward the other road. As in the poem, if we choose to take the less traveled road that follows Jesus, we anticipate that it will make all the difference.

Long before David Frost wrote his poem about two roads, Jesus gave a teaching about two roads: the broad road and the narrow road: *Enter through the narrow gate. For wide is the gate and broad is the road that leads to destruction, and many enter through it. But small is the gate and narrow the road that leads to life, and only a few find it* (Matthew 7:13-14). Notice that most people choose the broad road. That road obviously is not the one where people follow Jesus because it leads to destruction. The road where people follow Jesus leads to life, but that will be the road that fewer people travel.

Why would most people choose the broad road? It seems strange to us because we believe most people would choose life over death; yet, Jesus said that would not be the case. What factor would prompt the majority of people to choose a road that leads to death? Most people have a survival instinct that is within them since birth. When faced with death, we fight with all our energy, to the last moment, to stay alive. In many modern cultures, people go to great lengths to put off death. Consider how much money is spent on vitamins and medicines. Even aging is feared because it is a sign that we are moving closer to death. So gym memberships and plastic surgeries have become a part of life. Why indeed would most people choose the broad road over the narrow road, choosing death over life?

Jesus knew the reasons why and told us. It might shock you, but you might also relate. For one, not everyone wants to do the will of the Father in heaven (Matthew 7:21-23) because that would actually mean listening to Jesus's teachings and living by them (Matthew 7:24-27). They so prefer not following Jesus that they will join the majority on the broad road even though it will mean their death. Another reason is people fail to take time to consider Jesus, and having failed to do that, they fail to recognize they are on a road leading to death. They know nothing about the alternative road that Jesus offers, almost like that fork in the road is hidden from them. They do not even know it exists. They would, though, if they ever took the time to consider Jesus.

Can I offer you a personal observation? I am just one person, so I have limited knowledge and experience. Still, I have lived my share of years and have had some relevant experience. In my life, I have found that being religious often gets in the way of following Jesus. That sounds strange, doesn't it? We would think being part of some religious group, like a church or a denomination, would help us follow Jesus. Sadly, sometimes it becomes a hindrance. The church is indeed important, so we don't want to "throw the baby out with the bathwater" and stop being part of the church. We just need to be aware of the possible problem as we each reflect on following Jesus. This awareness can help us overcome the problem when it arises.

As you read this book, keep the picture of two roads, two choices, in your mind. Consider some additional questions: Will you follow Jesus, knowing it will bring you life? Or would you be so opposed to following Jesus that you would choose the broad road even though you know it will lead you to death? You stand at your fork in the road, and you have a choice to make. Your choice will make all the difference between life or death being your future. Will you follow Jesus, whatever that turns out to be? If your response is affirmative, then you have to understand a simple truth: *you can't follow Jesus unless you are on the same road He is on.* You see, following Jesus is really about roads. As you continue to read this book, you will learn more about the road that Jesus' followers take.

Pears and Avocados

A pear and an avocado. Two items that have some similarities. They are both green; they have the same basic shape. Both are fruits. If you were sent to the store to buy some pears, you would buy pears, not avocados. Why? Because they are not the same. You might like the taste of both, but some similarities do not make the two fruits the same item. Guacamole made with pears would not taste the same, nor would pear preserves taste good if avocados were used instead.

Is it possible that what is understood by many Christians to be a disciple is similar to what Jesus would say but actually is not the same? Looks can be deceiving, right? If we are going to make that determination one way or the other, it is important to first decide who defines what a disciple is, or who is a disciple.

Before we go too far down this road, I would offer that you need to buckle in for the journey. I do not say you should buckle in because we will be speeding on this journey. Rather, you need to buckle in so that you do not bail out. If you are going to be a disciple of Jesus, really be a disciple, you are going to want to bail on him multiple times. The only way to keep from bailing is to buckle yourself in tight. So do whatever you need to do to get securely buckled in. I will do what I can to help you.

Maybe we should start first with finding common ground on what is the basic understanding of a disciple in general. So let's take a little time with some basics. There are other words that are encompassed in *disciple,* such as *follower* and *student.*

To be a follower implies having a leader to follow. The follower imitates the leader, listens to, and obeys the leader. The follower goes where the leader goes or where the leader sends him or her. A follower submits to the authority of the leader, which means surrendering his or her will to the will of the leader.

To be a student requires a willingness to learn. That, in turn, implies newness and change. That change might be a change of direction, and it might mean a personal transformation. Very possibly, it can necessitate both. Learning requires an openness to new ideas, new attitudes, and new practices.

Combine these two concepts, and you see some important layers of being a disciple. You can't be a follower if you are not willing to learn new things. And what's the sense of learning new things if you do not do anything with the new, or if you are not changed by the new? These core elements of being a disciple will bring tension to life, though. Fundamentally, we humans do not naturally like change. We like sameness; we are comfortable with the status quo. While we have a desire to learn new things in our youth, the older we get, the more we hang on to what we already know.

Once I knew a man whose view of being a disciple had an inherent trap concealed in it. He was a husband and a father, and very good and conscientious about both. Still, he had a flaw in his thinking that tripped him up at times. When he viewed his connection to his church, he was open to any view or direction that he agreed with. However, if he disagreed with a view or a direction, he felt it was his role as a husband and a father to think and do otherwise. He saw this as protecting his family.

This sounds reasonable to us, but do you see the trap? When you start with the idea that you will follow a leader only as long as you agree, you've already unbuckled and prepared yourself to bail. We all sympathize with this man because we understand the rationale for not going along with things we do not agree with. Yet, it is important for us to recognize the tension that will arise when one decides to be a disciple of some leader. There will be many times when the follower does not agree with the leader and would prefer not to follow.

Consider how Jesus' teaching to turn the other cheek has seemed like nonsense to many who claim to be his disciples. Many would-be disciples have put any number of twists on his teaching to allow themselves room to actually disagree with the teaching and not follow Jesus when they disagree with him. Maybe you recall when you did exactly that. You may have eased the tension within you, but were you still following Jesus? Or did you actually bail?

Choosing to be a disciple of anybody is going to raise tension in one's life at some point. Will we accept new teachings, attitudes, and practices when we disagree? At the very least, we see clearly how important it is to choose the right leader if we are going to be a follower. Somehow, we have to find a way to resolve the tension of being a student and a follower when we disagree with the leader. If we are following a leader who is trustworthy and always right, this helps us follow even when we do not want to.

Now that we have laid out some basic concepts of being a disciple and recognized potential tensions, let's go a bit further. Who decides what it means to be a disciple of Jesus? The answer is obvious, right? Jesus is the leader, so he decides what it takes to be a disciple. He lays out the road a disciple must travel. That brings us back to the idea that we can't follow Jesus if we are not walking the same road.

Let's take a moment to consider this. If you are my leader and you decide to go from Chicago, Illinois to St. Louis, Missouri by walking southwest on Interstate 55, am I following you if I decide to walk east on Interstate 80? Will I even end up at the same destination? Of course not. We neither share the journey nor the experiences, and we end up in totally different locations. What if I decide to travel Interstate 55 like you, but I choose to drive my car? Am I following you? Of course not. I will get there long before you, and I will not have the same experiences. If I am going to follow you, my leader, I have to walk the same road you walk.

If we say Jesus is our leader, then he lays out for us the journey. He gives us the instruction, and we follow. He points us in new directions, and we follow them. He models a new attitude, and we imitate. He lays out the terms of being a disciple, not us. If we want to be a disciple of Jesus but are not comfortable with giving up control, we need to make sure we stay buckled in tightly. It is tempting to unbuckle, even though we are still in the car. We can already be thinking about when we will want to bail. If we are doing that, we are setting limits for how long we will follow our leader.

Now we have a fuller sense of what a disciple is and the surrender of will that is involved in being Jesus' disciple. This brings us to the focus of this book: where do we look for Jesus' instructions for his disciples? The obvious answer is, *we look to Jesus*. If this is as far as we go with that, however, we probably are the kind of people who go to the store for pears and come back with avocados. We might be disciples in some sense, but we risk finding out that we are not disciples of Jesus. We might have become disciples of a church or a religious heritage; or we might have become disciples of a persuasive preacher or the latest religious fad. We wrap our idea of discipleship in the name of Jesus and assume we are good to go, but are we?

Take a personal moment and reflect on why you are connected to the particular church that is in your life. Did you make that choice because of family heritage? Did you choose that church because a friend invited you? Are you there because you like the worship style or the preaching? Maybe these were people who helped you in your time of need. None of these are bad reasons for being part of a church; however, none of these reasons are focused on Jesus, are they? For your sake, go deeper to find a better reason to be part of a church. You may go deeper and not change your connection to that church. It is possible, though, that Jesus will point you elsewhere. Whatever the result, you decide whether or not you will follow Jesus. Pear or avocado?

In this book, we will put this thinking under the microscope and take a closer look. We will ask questions, and we will compare. We will determine if we have looked like disciples of Jesus but failed to become disciples of Jesus. So let me put you on alert: almost two thousand years have passed since Jesus called his first disciples so it is likely our view of discipleship has been warped in some way. We might even find that we haven't even been on the same road as Jesus. If being a disciple involves learning and adjusting, take whatever you learn and make the changes you need to make. If you do that, you will be back on the right road of following Jesus.

The microscope we will use is found in the gospel of Matthew. You can use Mark, Luke, and John as well, but we will focus on Matthew. So let's get out our microscope. In 1946, a man named Jack Dean Kingsbury wrote about this microscope. He identified five places in Matthew's gospel where Jesus was instructing primarily his disciples about following him. There is a key phrase that marks the end of each of these teachings: *when Jesus had finished saying these things*. You will find that phrase, or some variant of it, in Matthew 7:28; 11:1; 13:53; 19:1; and 26:1. These are markers that let the reader know that Jesus had finished some teaching.

There is more to know about these sections of teaching. If you work backwards to where the teachings start, or near the start, you will find who Jesus was teaching. So working backwards, you will find this information in 5:1; 10:1; 13:1-2, 10; 18:1; and 24:1, 3. Who was Jesus' audience in these teachings? Sometimes the crowds were present; always, his disciples were present. As you read each section of teaching, it becomes clear that Jesus' disciples were his primary focus. In these sections, Jesus is teaching his disciples how to be disciples.

When it comes to walking the same road as Jesus, it is critical that we grasp this. Why? Go to the end of Matthew's gospel and read the words of Jesus to his disciples that are recorded in *Matthew 28:18-20*:

> *Then Jesus came to them and said, "All authority in heaven and on earth has been given to me. Therefore go and make disciples of all nations, baptizing them in the name of the Father and of the Son and of the Holy Spirit, and teaching them to obey everything I have commanded you."*

Christians know this text very well and often refer to it as *The Great Commission*. What exactly did Jesus say in his commission to his first disciples? Remember, Jesus is the one who leads, and he determines what makes someone a disciple, so we need to make sure we get this and follow him. Primarily, he sent those men to make other disciples. That is the leading verb of his commission. This verb is followed by two subordinate verbs that give instruction on how to do that.

First, Jesus said new disciples needed to be baptized in the name of the Father, Son, and Spirit. *Baptize* actually means *immerse*. That is the first step, according to Jesus, in making disciples. This may be a new insight for you. Perhaps you were not taught that Jesus required you to be immersed in water. Maybe you learned something that was shaped by almost two thousand years of Christian religion. What I share with you is straight from Jesus, and if you let him be your North Star, you will be just fine.

The second verb instructed his disciples to teach others what Jesus taught them. These new disciples-in-making would need to obey those teachings. Followers can't follow their leader if they do not know what their leader has taught, wouldn't you agree? Yet a truth so simple may have been almost completely missed. Why? Because many have failed to see those teachings even though they have read them. How is that possible? I will explain.

To be sure, there are teachings of Jesus in all four gospels that we need to hear and obey. There are also teachings of Jesus throughout Matthew's gospel that we need to hear and obey. We should not miss any of those. However, if Matthew identifies five places where Jesus spoke specifically, sometimes even solely, to his disciples about being his disciple, doesn't it make sense that we should look very closely there? That is what we will do in this book, and those five sections of teachings in Matthew's gospel will be our microscope.

This seems pretty simple and straightforward, doesn't it? Yet many Christians do not even know about these five sections of teaching. I knew about them for years as a preacher, but I did not connect the dots like I should have. I baptized people into Jesus many times, but I did not teach those new disciples what Jesus taught in those five sections of teaching. Preachers and churches have been developing discipleship material for ages, maybe since the early days of the church. Yet how many discipleship classes and programs never even touch these five sections of teaching from Jesus? Remember, these are sections where the leader, Jesus, is teaching his followers, people like us, how to follow him. They are pretty important for that reason.

Now might be a good time to pause and reflect on the teaching you have received. Did you even know about these five blocks of teaching and their significance? Have you and others spent time with those teachings from Jesus? If you have, wonderful! If you haven't, what have you missed? If we have not spent time learning these teachings then maybe we are not following them, If that is the case, perhaps we are not even following Jesus. Maybe we are walking a different road altogether. Maybe we have been avocados and not pears. If that has happened, we need to find out, and the sooner, the better.

Before we step into the first section, though, we will do a seat belt check. We will do that regularly on our journey down this road of following Jesus. It just might help us not bail.

Seat Belt Check

Seat belts do not do much good if we are not buckled in tight. This is true with traveling in a car; it is true with following Jesus. Jesus is so radically different from this world, that we must expect him to lead us into some difficult teachings and circumstances. To help you stay tight with Jesus, I offer you this seat belt check.

If I asked you, *Do you believe the Bible is true and should be followed?,* you likely would say, *Yes.*

If I asked you, *Do you have a complete and perfect understanding of the Bible?,* you likely would say, *No.*

If you answered both questions as I assumed you would, then you are acknowledging something that you likely have not considered until now. You are saying that you now believe something in the Bible that is wrong. You probably did not see that coming, so think about it. If you do not have a perfect understanding of the Bible, then that means some understanding you have is wrong. That means somewhere you have a wrong belief. Don't get too upset about that, though, because we all have this problem.

Go a step further: if I ask you, *Can you tell me what it is that you currently believe that is wrong?* You would be unable to because if you knew something was wrong, you would have already changed it. You are a conscientious person, and you do not deliberately hang on to something that is false. Since you will never have a perfect understanding of the Bible, that means you will always have some wrong belief.

What can you do about this? I suggest two things. First, do not get stressed out, because this is the state that every person finds themselves in, even a disciple. Second, do not be afraid to acknowledge you are wrong when you find out. It is okay to admit you are wrong. Not a lot of people are comfortable with that, but we would all be better off if we were. When it comes to following Jesus, you are going to find, perhaps quite often, that your understanding is wrong. Just be a student, recognize what is wrong, learn and change, and then move forward. This is how we get further down the road with Jesus.

That concludes our seat belt check. You are buckled in tight when you know it is just fine when you recognize you are wrong in some understanding of following Jesus. When you recognize that, make the changes you need to make and trust Jesus; you are going to be better off with the understanding that he will give you. Be glad you get to be rid of your wrong understanding and take on his perfect understanding.

Matthew 5-7
First Block of Teaching

5 Now when Jesus saw the crowds, he went up on a mountainside and sat down. His disciples came to him, ² and he began to teach them.

³" Blessed are the poor in spirit, for theirs is the kingdom of God.

⁴ Blessed are those who mourn, for they will be comforted.

⁵ Blessed are the meek, for they will inherit the earth.

⁶ Blessed are those who hunger and thirst for righteousness, for they will be filled.

⁷ Blessed are the merciful, for they will be shown mercy.

⁸ Blessed are the pure in heart, for they will see God.

⁹ Blessed are the peacemakers, for they will be called children of God.

¹⁰ Blessed are those who are persecuted because of righteousness, for theirs is the kingdom of heaven.

¹¹ "Blessed are you when people insult you, persecute you and falsely say all kinds of evil against you because of me. ¹² Rejoice and be glad, because great is your reward in heaven, for in the same way they persecuted the prophets who were before you.

¹³ "You are the salt of the earth, but if the salt loses its saltiness, how can it be made salty again? It is no longer good for anything except to be thrown out and trampled underfoot.

[14] "You are the light of the world. A town built on a hill cannot be hidden. [15] Neither do people light a lamp and put it under a bowl. Instead they put it on its stand, and it gives light to everyone in the house. [16] In the same way, let your light shine before others, so that they may see your good deeds and glorify your Father in heaven.

[17] "Do not think that I have come to abolish the Law or the Prophets; I did not come to abolish them but to fulfill them. [18] For truly I tell you, until heaven or earth disappear, not the smallest letter, not the least stroke of a pen, will by any means disappear from the Law until everything is accomplished. [19] Therefore anyone who sets aside one of the least of these commands and teaches others accordingly will be called least in the kingdom of heaven, but whoever practices and teaches these commands will be called great in the kingdom of heaven. [20] For I tell you that unless your righteousness surpasses that of the Pharisees and the teachers of the law, you will never enter the kingdom of heaven.

[21] "You have heard that it was said to the people long ago, 'You shall not murder, and anyone who murders will be subject to judgment.' [22] But I tell you that anyone who is angry with his brother or sister will be subject to judgment. Again, anyone who says to his brother or sister, 'Raca,' is answerable to the court. And anyone who says, 'You fool!' will be in danger of the fire of hell.

[23] "Therefore, if you are offering your gift at the altar and there remember that your brother or sister has something against you, [24] leave your gift at the altar. First go to be reconciled with your brother or sister, and then come and offer your gift.

²⁵ "Settle matters quickly with your adversary who is taking you to court. Do it while you are still together on the way, or your adversary may hand you over to the judge, and the judge hand you over to the officer, and you may be thrown into prison. ²⁶ Truly I tell you, you will not get out until you have paid the last penny.

²⁷ "You have heard, 'You shall not commit adultery.' ²⁸ But I tell you that anyone who looks at a woman lustfully has already committed adultery with her in his heart. ²⁹ If your right eye causes you to stumble, gouge it out and throw it away. It is better for you to lose one part of your body than for your whole body to be thrown into hell. ³⁰ If your right hand causes you to stumble, cut it off and throw it away. It is better for you to lose one part of your body than for your whole body to go into hell.

³¹ "It has been said, 'Anyone who divorces his wife must give her a certificate of divorce. ³² But I tell you that anyone who divorces his wife, except for sexual immorality, makes her a victim of adultery, and anyone who marries the divorced woman commits adultery.

³³"Again, you have heard that it was said to the people long ago, 'Do not break your oath, but fulfill to the Lord the vows you have made.' ³⁴ But I tell you, do not swear an oath at all; either by heaven, for it is God's throne; ³⁵or by the earth for it is his footstool; or by Jerusalem, for it is the city of the Great King. ³⁶ And do not swear by your head, for you cannot make even one hair white or black. ³⁷ All you need to say is simply 'Yes' or 'No'; anything beyond this comes from the evil one.

[38] "You have heard that it was said, 'Eye for eye, and tooth for tooth.' [39] But I tell you, do not resist an evil person. If anyone slaps you on the right cheek, turn to them the other cheek also. [40] And if anyone wants to sue you and take your shirt, hand over your coat as well. [41] If anyone forces you to go one mile, go with them two miles. [42] Give to the one who asks you, and do no turn away from the one who wants to borrow from you.

[43] "You have heard that it was said, 'Love your neighbor and hate your enemy. [44] But I tell you, love your enemies and pray for those who persecute you, [45] that you may be children of your Father in heaven. He causes his sun to rise on the evil and good, and sends rain on the righteous and unrighteous. [46] If you love those who love you, what reward will you get? Are not even tax collectors doing that? [47] And if you greet only your own people, what are you doing more than others? Do not even pagans do that? [48] Be perfect, therefore, as your heavenly Father is perfect.

6 "Be careful not to do your acts of righteousness in front of others to be seen by them. If you do, you will have no reward from your Father in heaven.

[2] "So when you give to the needy, do not announce it with trumpets as the hypocrites do in the synagogues and on the streets to be honored by others. Truly I tell you, they have received their reward in full. [3] But when you give to the needy, do not let your left hand know what your right hand is doing, [4] so that your giving may done in secret. Then your Father, who sees what is done in secret, will reward you.

5 "And when you pray, do not be like the hypocrites, who like to pray standing in the synagogues and on the street corners to be seen by others. Truly I tell you, they have received their reward in full. 6 But when you pray, go into your room, close the door and pray to your Father, who is unseen. Then your Father, who sees what is done in secret, will reward you. 7 And when you pray, do not keep on babbling like pagans, for they think they will be heard because of their many words. 8 Do not be like them, for your Father knows what you need before you ask him.

9 "This, then, is how you should pray:"'Our Father in heaven, hallowed be your name, 10 your kingdom come, your will be done, on earth as it is in heaven.

11 Give us today our daily bread.

12 And forgive us our debts, as we also have forgiven our debtors.

13 And lead us not into temptation, but deliver us from the evil one.

14 For if you forgive other people when they sin against you, your heavenly Father will also forgive you. 15 But if you do not forgive others their sins, your Father will not forgive your sins.

16 "When you fast, do not look somber as the hypocrites do, for they disfigure their faces to show others they are fasting. Truly I tell you, they have received their reward in full. 17 But when you fast, put oil on your head and wash your face, 18 so that it will not be obvious to others that you are fasting, but only to your Father who is unseen; and your Father who sees what is done in secret will reward you.

[19] "Do not store up for yourselves treasures on earth where moths and vermin destroy, and where thieves break in and steal. [20] But store up for yourselves treasures in heaven, where moths and vermin do not destroy, and where thieves do no break in and steal. [21] For where your treasure is, there your heart will be also.

[22] "The eye is the lamp of the body. If your eyes are healthy, your whole body will be full of light. [23] But if your eyes are unhealthy, your whole body will be full of darkness. If then the light within you is darkness, how great is that darkness?

[24] "No one can serve two masters. Either you will hate the one and love the other, or you will be devoted to one and despise the other. You cannot serve both God and money.

[25] "Therefore, I tell you, do not worry about your life, what you will eat or drink; or about your body; what you will wear. Is not life more than food, and the body more than clothes? [26] Look at the birds of the air, they do not sow, or reap, or store away in barns, and yet your heavenly Father feeds them. Are you not much more valuable than they? [27] Can anyone of you by worrying can add single hour to your life?

[28] "And why do you worry about clothes? See how the flowers of the field grow. They do not labor or spin. [29] Yet I tell you that not even Solomon in all of his splendor was dressed like one of these. [30] If that is how God clothes the grass of the field, which is here today and tomorrow is thrown into the fire, will he not much more clothe you — you of little faith? [31] So do not worry, saying, 'What shall we eat?' or 'What shall we drink?' or 'What shall we wear?' [32] For the pagans run after all these

things, and your heavenly Father knows that you need them. [33] But seek first his kingdom and his righteousness, and all these things will be given to you as well. [34] Therefore, do not worry about tomorrow, for tomorrow will take care of itself. Each day has enough trouble of its own.

[7] "Do not judge, or you too will be judged. [2] For in the same way you judge others, you will be judged, and with the measure you use, it will be measured to you.

[3] "Why do you look at the speck of sawdust in your brother's eye and pay no attention to the plank in your own eye? [4] How can you say to your brother, 'Let me take the speck out of your eye, when all the time there is a plank in your own eye? [5] You hypocrite, first take the speck out of your own eye, then you will see clearly to remove the speck from your brother's eye.

[6] Do not give dogs what is sacred; do not throw your pearls to pigs. If you do, they may trample them under their feet, and turn and tear you to pieces.

[7] "Ask and it will be given to you; seek and you will find; knock and the door will be opened to you. [8] For everyone who asks receives; the one who seeks will find; and to the one who knocks, the door will be opened.

[9] "Which of you, if your son asks for bread, will give him a stone? [10] Or if he asks you for a fish, will give him a snake? [11] If you, then, though you are evil, know how to give good gifts to your children, how much more will your Father in heaven give good gifts to these who ask

him? [12] So in everything, do to others as you would have them do to you, for this sums up the Law and the Prophets.

[13] "Enter through the narrow gate, for wide is the gate and broad is the road that leads to destruction, and many enter through it. [14] But small is the gate, and narrow the road that leads to life, and only a few find it.

[15] "Watch out for false prophets. They come to you in sheep's clothing, but inwardly they are ferocious wolves. [16] By their fruit, you will recognize them. Do people pick grapes from thornbushes, or figs from thistles? [17]Likewise, every good tree bears good fruit, but a bad tree bears bad fruit. [18] A good tree cannot bear bad fruit, and a bad tree cannot bear good fruit. [19] Every tree that does not bear good fruit is cut down and thrown into the fire. [20] Thus, by their fruit you will recognize them.

[21] "Not everyone who says to me, 'Lord, Lord,' will enter the kingdom of heaven, but only the one who does the will of my Father who is in heaven. [22] Many will say to me on that day, 'Lord, Lord, did we not prophesy in your name and in your name drive out demons and perform many miracles.' [23] Then I will tell them plainly, 'I never knew you. Away from me, you evildoers!'

[24] "Therefore, everyone who hears these words of mine and puts them into practice is like a wise man who built his house on the rock. [25] The rain came down, the streams rose, and the winds blew and beat against that house; yet it did not fall, because it had its foundation on the rock. [26] But everyone who hears these words of mine and does not put them into practice is like a foolish man who built his house on sand. [27]

The rain came down, the streams rose, and the wind blew and beat against that house, and it fell with a great crash.

[28] When Jesus had finished saying these things, the crowds were amazed at his teaching, because he taught them as one who had authority, and not as their teachers of the law.

Prepping for the Teaching

Likely, you have heard or read this section of Jesus' teachings before, or at least some of it. Many famous sayings have been drawn from these teachings, often referred to as *The Sermon on the Mount*. Perhaps you are used to worshiping in church buildings and hearing sermons; you might think this does not sound like any sermon you have ever heard from a modern preacher. It might help you to know that Jesus delivered his teachings in ways that rabbis often did; for example, rabbis would often sit down when they taught their disciples. But we are not using our microscope to understand the form of Jesus' teaching. We want to examine what he taught his disciples about following him and compare what we learn to what we see people living out. We especially want to see how our lives as disciples compare to what Jesus has taught.

We will not look at the whole section of teaching in one chunk. If we did that, we would choke on it like people taking too big of a bite of food in their meal. Nor will we look at it verse by verse; if we did that, you would likely lose interest, and this book would turn into volumes of books. What I propose to do is give you insights into sections of the teaching that are manageable and that can equip you for a closer, more detailed look on your own.

Take some time to read the whole section of teaching at least once, more if you want. We are in no rush, so read it as many times as you want or need to get familiar with it. I have put the whole section on these pages for that purpose so that you can go back and look it over as we proceed. When you are ready, come back here, and we will begin.

The Thread that Runs Through

As you read, you picked up on some hard teachings about two groups of people that were very powerful and prominent in Israel - Pharisees and teachers of the law. These were the religious leaders of Israel, much like preachers and pastors are in our society. You noticed that everything Jesus said about them in his teachings was negative. He was no fan of theirs.

Allow me to take you back to some of the things he said about those people. Jesus accused them of not practicing or teaching all of the Law and the Prophets (the Bible of Israel). He also told the disciples and the people who wanted to be in his kingdom that in order to even get into the kingdom, they had to reach a level of righteousness that exceeded what they saw or heard from the Pharisees and teachers of the law. Jesus apparently did not see many of them even getting into the kingdom of heaven. He instructed the people and his disciples to look instead to the Father in heaven for their role model; he is the perfect role model.

You heard several times from Jesus, "You have heard it said…but I tell you." That was Jesus contrasting his teachings with what the Pharisees and teachers of the law were teaching the Israelites. Some of their teachings were wrong because they did not understand the heart of the Law and Prophets. Sometimes they were wrong because they inserted applications that were not in the scriptures, but their applications fit into their comfort zone.

At the end of this section of Jesus' teachings, you heard him talk about wolves

in sheep's clothing and trees with bad fruit. You also heard him talk about people who would call him Lord and who would call themselves followers because they were pretty good at doing religious things. What did Jesus say would be their reward? Fire. Total rejection from Jesus. If you have understood this as harsh judgment from Jesus on the Pharisees and teachers of the law, you have understood correctly.

Even that initial crowd and those first disciples understood. They saw the difference between the teachings of Jesus and their religious leaders. They recognized even then who had the real authority.

Seeing this thread is critical, but it is only the first thing you need to do. Now you need to compare. You can compare the religious leaders of today with those Pharisees and teachers of the law. Perhaps you will identify modern wolves in sheep's clothing. If you do, you now know to avoid them. Not everyone who sets themselves up as religious leaders, even those who call Jesus their Lord, are necessarily his followers. Jesus said, if you look closely enough, you will be able to tell because you will see bad fruit in their lives and ministries.

You can take your comparisons further. If you have a religious background or continue in your faith tradition, you might find yourself on the path of the Pharisees rather than the path Jesus set. When we follow the wrong leader, we take on their qualities, and their values, their attitudes, not Jesus'. We can find ourselves on the wrong side of Jesus' evaluation. Even today, there are competing voices with Jesus. Those voices can be church leaders such as preachers, pastors, or priests. Every would-be disciple has a responsibility to make sure such people are actually following Jesus themselves.

How do I find out if I am in danger here? How do I stay on my guard and still keep the heart and mind of a disciple who is willing to learn new things? A pretty good way to do that is to just spend time with Jesus' teachings, with no middle person. Meditate on them, get familiar with them. Pray over them. You are at the source of truth when you do this, and good things can happen.

Then consider how Jesus' teachings impacted you as you read them. Did you recoil or struggle with any, maybe several? Did you find yourself dismissing any teaching? Did you find yourself out of step with Jesus anywhere? If you did, write down the teachings you were uncomfortable with. Then take some time to reflect on what you have heard from whoever took you down a different road. It is possible that you have been listening to the wrong voice. If so, you have some evaluating to do and some tough choices ahead. You can choose to change and actually follow Jesus, or you can choose to stay your course. The latter choice will not end well for you. You get to choose, just like anyone who wants to follow Jesus. Unfortunately, the right choices are not always the easy choices.

Kingdom People and Kingdom Values (5:3-12)

Let's move into the teachings of Jesus now. Jesus began his teachings with the Beatitudes, a series of statements that redefined who is truly blessed in the kingdom of God. These were radical in the first-century Jewish context, challenging societal norms and religious expectations of who was considered righteous and favored by God. These *beatitudes* give us a window into the values the King is looking for in his followers. They are not values that are generally promoted by society or culture. From the beginning, Jesus wants those who want to be his disciples to know they will be following a leader who is going to turn the world on its head. Perhaps these statements were not intended by Jesus to be fully understood, but rather to prepare followers to be radically different from their social circles and culture.

We should be sure to not miss which beatitude Jesus elaborated on. It was not enough for Jesus to just hold up the value of willingly suffering for the kingdom, he homed in on that value. *Do you want to be a disciple? Do you realize it will mean suffering at many levels? Are you ready to sign up for that?*

Perhaps this causes us to pause, and rightfully so. If Jesus is going to give us blessings, why wouldn't we sign up for that? But if following Jesus will bring us into hatred and persecution, why would we sign up for that? If your idea of following Jesus is some form of comfortable Christianity, then Jesus is challenging your thinking already. He will go even further with this in other sections of his teaching. For Jesus, the idea of his disciples suffering is not a possibility. It is a certainty. Will you follow Jesus down that road?

It is possible that you live in a place where the only price you have had to pay for following Jesus is losing some morning sleep so that you could be on time for going to an hour of worship. So what Jesus spoke about in this block of teaching is radically different. In other places, not so safe, followers of Jesus are separated from family, imprisoned, tortured, and killed. As humans, we tend to think of the followers living in comfort and safety as the more fortunate. Yet in a kingdom that is counter-culture, Jesus knows the high cost of following him and still calls his disciples to make that sacrifice. So now is a good time to consider what in your life is worth the ultimate sacrifice. It could help you to talk this out with others who are also considering following Jesus.

Stark Contrast (5:13-16)

As we move further into Jesus' teaching, salt and light are used to illustrate for his listeners that being his disciple is not a matter of being marginally, slightly, or microscopically different from one's society. To be his disciple would so radically change a person that an unmistakable, marked difference would make that disciple stand out from all around him or her. Just like how salt would make food taste dramatically different, or how a light would stand out from the darkness. Salt and light that do not do that are useless. So is the disciple who fails to stand out from the culture he or she lives in.

Jesus takes us into an understanding that following him threatens a core element of culture, any culture. Culture embraces conformity. Every culture is built on the concept that a certain number of people are so similar in what they value that they can and do choose to live together. They establish a norm and live comfortably within it. Divergence from this norm threatens that culture because divergence challenges the status quo and seeks to change it. No earthly culture aligns with kingdom of heaven values; therefore, the kingdom of heaven is a divergent threat to any culture. Even cultures that profess to be Christian have been corrupted by other values; the result is there is no human culture that truly reflects the kingdom. Do not expect the culture you live in to ever fully embrace the values of the kingdom of heaven. Expect the time to come when you will have to pay some price for refusing to conform.

If you have been a professed follower of Jesus for any length of time, reflect on that time of your baptism when you made your commitment. Were you excited about joining a dynamic church that offered lots of cool opportunities for friendship, community, and cheery worship services? Were you relieved that you were escaping a death sentence in hell? Were you thrilled to know you were joining your friends, and you would be part of their group of believers? I raise these questions because they speak to why many people decide to follow Jesus. How do those reasons square with Jesus' teachings about being hated and persecuted? What will happen to your commitment when such opposition stares you in the face? Maybe now is a good time to start preparing for and praying about what Jesus said is sure to come. Maybe now is a good time to start developing a disciple's mindset when faced with persecution and hatred.

If you haven't made a decision to follow Jesus yet, then you are hearing what Jesus wants you to know on the front end. He is calling you into a blessed life, a full life, and indeed the best life. However, do not mistake that for a comfortable life. Surely you will have times of great comfort, and God will love to bless you with as much as he can. That does not change the fact, though, that disciples of Jesus are choosing to walk a different road from the culture in which they live. Diverge down that road and culture will make you pay for that choice. Jesus wants you to say yes to him because he knows that will be the best for you, but he also wants you to know the cost upfront.

Where the Rubber Meets the Road (5:17-6:34)

It is one thing to speak in vague or theoretical terms. If you want to draw large crowds and gain a huge following, the prevailing practice is to avoid getting pinned down; don't say anything that will offend or that you will have to walk back. Nobody told that to Jesus. He wanted followers, but he wanted them to follow values that were not cloaked in foggy rhetoric. His followers could not live out his values if they did not know them, so he plainly put them out there for all to hear.

First, he let those would-be disciples know that his teachings were just a continuation of what the Father in heaven had already laid out. However, his teachings would go all the way to the heart and not stop at traditions, comfort zones, or cultural preferences. He drew a line in the sand that defined a major shift between him and the religious leaders of those people. They had so badly missed the teachings of the Father in heaven that they would not even make it into the kingdom. Whoever wanted to enter the kingdom had to go well beyond the religious leaders' teachings and follow Jesus' teachings. He raised the bar higher than anyone had ever seen.

Then Jesus proceeded to touch on six areas of life where religious leaders had set the bar too low: anger, lust, devaluing marriage, not keeping your word, vengeance, and treatment of enemies. Don't think Jesus just pulled these six topics out of a hat. He had seen how people were living. He had heard how they had been taught in their religious assemblies. He knew when and how they would bend the teachings of God to suit themselves.

The norm was to draw the line on murder; Jesus drew the line at anger and called his disciples to put reconciliation at the top of their to-do list. The norm was to draw the line at married men sneaking around and sleeping with other women; Jesus drew the line at just thinking about it and fantasizing about it, calling men to honor their wives. The norm drew the line at divorcing wives for trivial reasons and putting their ex-wives in situations of breaking the covenant themselves; Jesus drew the line at honoring marriage covenants and working through problems. The norm was to draw the line at only keeping your word if you made a binding vow; Jesus drew the line at being honest and forthright, keeping your word no matter how much it cost you. The norm was to draw the line of vengeance at causing no more hurt than what you received; Jesus drew the line at forgiving others when wronged and still helping those who wronged you. The norm drew the line of love to extend no further than those you liked and endorsed hatred of enemies. Jesus drew no line when it came to love; he taught to love everybody, even enemies.

When Jesus finished these six teachings, he sealed them with the highest standard: set your eyes on the Father in heaven and try to be like him. Don't settle for what the religious leaders have been teaching you. No longer live like the people around you, no matter how many rabbis and teachers support you; live above the world and live out God's values.

How many of those would-be disciples had been on the wrong side of some situation where they got burned by the cultural values? These words of Jesus were exciting and set their minds racing; what could life be like for them if they were followers of Jesus and lived by his values? Surely they also reflected on when they had been on the right side of cultural values and came out the loser. The words of Jesus had to convict them and challenge them. Was it possible to live up to such a high standard in a broken culture? Could anyone really live out God's values in the midst of people who cared only for themselves and their own? Jesus believed his disciples could.

Let's take a moment to compare our lives now with the teachings of the one we claim to follow. Do we believe we can live up to the standard Jesus set for his followers? If we want to call ourselves disciples, will we set our eyes on God and not people? I have met many godly preachers through the years and have been blessed by them. I have also met another type. I knew a preacher at one point in my life who hired bodyguards to protect him; he was also known for sleeping with the women in the church where he preached. There was probably a connection between these two aspects of his life. I knew a married man who loved being in the spotlight in a church while living with another woman when his work sent him out of town. I knew a church that loved having a woman as a member because she was such a powerful and beautiful singer, while they turned a blind eye to her living with a man to whom she was not married and having a child with him. Does any of this sound familiar to you?

There have been churches where the color of a person's skin prevented them from being allowed to worship there. I have been in churches where anger and judgment broke friendships and led to name-calling, dissension, and division. I have been in churches where comfort was so solidified in the people's spiritual DNA that sacrifice and enduring persecution were unthinkable and avoided at all costs. I have seen people who called themselves followers of Jesus who looked so much like their culture that being like Jesus became little more than being a nice person. Have you experienced this as well?

Perhaps my experience is limited and not indicative of reality. Or perhaps my experiences are just the tip of a nasty iceberg. It is not my place or role to sit in judgment on others, lest I become guilty of not following Jesus myself because of a judgmental spirit. My role is simply to point out comparisons so that we can make the changes that need to be made. If we realize we have somehow ended up on the wrong road, we can find the right road and get on it.

You and I might think that Jesus had said enough by this point in his teachings, and we might want a chance to breathe. If you need to pause for a bit to absorb these teachings, go ahead and pause. Reflect and pray over what is challenging you, but do not stop. Be sure to come back and hear all of Jesus' teachings. Hang on to the truth that following Jesus is where you will find kingdom life.

When you are ready to press on, we will consider how Jesus challenged one of the sacred cows of his culture—honor. The people of Israel, especially the men, highly valued honor. Matthew Neyrey wrote about this in his book, Honor and Shame in Matthew's Gospel. All the men wanted honor, so they would use whatever culturally acceptable means they could to get it. If people recognized them for doing honorable things like giving to the poor, praying, and fasting, or by some other means, then they would get more honor.

As a result, people might find themselves tripping over those praying loudly and obnoxiously at street corners. Or they could find themselves being stopped while trumpets blasted as some honor-seeking person pulled out a few coins to toss to a beggar. Or they could possibly find themselves coming face-to-face with their rabbi, who that day was wearing rags because he wanted everyone to see his piety as he fasted. It was all a sham, a show put on by men seeking nothing more than being honored by the people.

You can hear the voices of the people: "What a godly man!" "Oh, how generous our rabbi was when he gave that poor beggar some money. The beggar will probably misspend it, but that's on him. Our rabbi can't do more than he did. What a godly man." "Did you see our rabbi yesterday and hear his beautiful prayer at the marketplace? So forceful and humble at the same time." "My, my, our poor rabbi was terribly vexed the other day. I don't know what was troubling him, but it had to be something bad for him to be dressed in those filthy, shredded clothes. That isn't how he dresses for synagogue on Sabbath, thank goodness. Well, at least he made his point, and I hope people were watching and learned."

Jesus slammed it all for what it was. He put his would-be disciples on notice that the Father in heaven would not give honor to such behavior. He valued what was unseen, what was truly in one's heart, where lay the real motivation behind such acts. He was able to see what rewards and treasures people really desired. Using the needs of others to lift up oneself or using the act of humbling oneself before God as a step ladder to advance in society was completely out of bounds to the Father in heaven. He would not be fooled by such hypocrisy.

When we compare Jesus' teachings to our own times, surely the pursuit of personal honor has not distorted the way people profess to follow Jesus today. Then again, maybe it is still a sacred cow. I have known preachers who sacrificed much to share God's message with people others had walked away from. I have also seen a preacher chastise other preachers to make sure their members contributed monetarily to his special day of being honored and blessed financially, threatening not to support other preachers on their special days if they failed to support his. I have seen a preacher brag about his car not starting and not being able to get under the car to fix it because he was wearing a very expensive suit. However, he had no problem with a member of his church getting his Sunday clothes dirty to fix his car. It seems modern Christian leaders can struggle with honor as well.

Honor is not just a trap that catches preachers, though. How many church members are more prone to sign up for acts of service that put them in the spotlight while shunning the dirtier, menial acts of love that do not get attention? Have you ever been in a church where there was never a problem getting people to volunteer for leading in public worship or planning special parties, but getting people to volunteer to help in the nursery or Children's Church required weekly announcements, prodding, guilt-tripping, and eventually drafting? Yes, honor from the wrong places, attained in the wrong ways, is still a treasure that many would-be disciples set their hearts on.

That thought of treasure led Jesus into the next value he wanted his disciples to embrace. His disciples needed to be focused on righteousness, not the pursuit of money. We should note that Jesus did not say *riches*; he said *money*. Jesus looked at his culture and saw that the righteousness of God, the Father's values, was not the typical pursuit of people. They were consumed with the pursuit of money, rich and poor alike. Some had plenty and wanted more; others had little or none and were trying to get enough to provide for their family. The result for both was the all-out pursuit of money by whatever means necessary, no matter what people or values got sacrificed in the pursuit.

How did Jesus address that? Was there one message for the wealthy, who could pull back their pursuit some and still eat at night in warm houses? Was there another message for the poor and homeless, or nearly homeless, who may have been just a few coins away from starving? No. Jesus had the same message for both: stop living like people who do not trust God. If you say you trust God, then trust him. Commit to living by his values, and trust him to meet your needs. He will. If you need proof, look at the birds and the flowers. Your Father will provide for your daily needs; don't let your worries about tomorrow consume you today.

Jesus' teachings on money present significant challenges. Like the early disciples, modern readers may struggle with the radical call to trust in God's provision rather than worldly wealth. Trusting God with religion is one thing; trusting him with the bills and daily needs is a much higher level of trust. Can we do that? If so, what does this look like?

People feel financial pressure to cover two needs: today's and tomorrow's. It is easy to become anxious about either. Unrelenting concern about both can dominate a person's life and be a constant source of anxiety. This anxiety can drive a person to a never-ending pursuit of money, revealing that money has become a cruel master or a god to the person. Jesus offers release from such servitude.

How does a disciple apply Jesus' teaching so that anxiety does not mount over financial concerns and money does not become a god? Two viewpoints come to my mind; both have been lived out by people who want to live as disciples. One viewpoint promotes financial planning, saving money responsibly, and planning for retirement. Money is not a god, but it is seen as a necessity that needs to be thought about and budgeted responsibly. This will enable a disciple to live without financial anxiety and use money not only to pay bills but also to bless others as well. There are many believers who subscribe to this viewpoint.

The other viewpoint promotes a greater dependence on God, so much so that one does not set aside money for retirement. Instead, a disciple relies more on God's provisions for today's needs; this disciple trusts that when tomorrow becomes today, God will provide for those needs as well. This viewpoint seems extremely radical to many current disciples. Perhaps one of the more noted examples of living by this viewpoint was a disciple, George Mueller, who lived in the 1800s to early 1900s. He never asked a person for any money—not as a minister, not even when he and his wife took on caring for orphans or supporting missionaries worldwide. One glimpse of his life reveals that he and those who joined him took care of ten thousand orphans in his lifetime, providing housing, clothing, meals, and all necessities. They never asked for any money from anyone, only asking God to meet their needs. No need went unmet. George Mueller kept a record of fifteen thousand prayers answered during his life; five thousand were answered on the same day the prayers were lifted up. His life story is worth reading.

Both viewpoints have their proponents. The second is definitely more challenging, but it also offers a greater opportunity to experience God because the disciple can see how God meets daily needs, just as Jesus said he would. Whatever viewpoint one has on money, Jesus informs his disciples that money cannot be their master. Every disciple has to find a way that follows the teacher in this part of life.

It All Boils Down to This (Matthew 7:1-12)

When people practice religion by comparing themselves to others, they will ultimately end up judging one another. Who is doing better at being religious? Who is viewed by others as doing well? And who is failing miserably when they think no one is looking? The only way for someone in that cycle to feel good about themselves is to see others as doing worse. *"Well, at least I am not as bad as..."*

Jesus did not lay out his teachings for his disciples to keep walking as they had on their former road. To prevent that, he sums up his teachings with some good pointers. Again, Jesus taught a radical view that produces radical transformation.

First, just don't judge others. Realize you are messing up too, so be humble enough to see your need to change and work on it. When you have figured out how to walk the road of a disciple, then you can help the other person. So stay away from judging.

Second, don't rely on *dogs* and *pigs* to help you be a disciple. This is a puzzling teaching, but that is what Jesus said, so let's take some time to understand his words. Remember, his message was to instruct would-be followers on how to actually be followers. What does that have to do with dogs and pigs? The Jews had a habit of looking down on people who were not Jewish. They considered them to be no better than dogs. In fact, they would call them dogs. Non-Jewish people (Gentiles) were also people who had no problem raising and eating pigs. Those Gentiles were uncultured swine! Connect the dots: Jesus is instructing his followers not to look to the pagan culture to help them understand the principles of living as his follower. The pagans would not understand why Jesus' followers would even try to live by those values; in fact, not only would they not understand, but the pagans would also even use those values against his disciples.

An illustration of this can be taken from Jesus' teaching about turning the other cheek. Suppose a disciple went to a Roman landlord and informed him that he was short of money and needed an extension. The disciple rested his hope on the landlord being understanding and merciful. However, the landlord knew his tenant was a follower of Jesus, and instead of helping, he saw the opportunity to not only insult and mock his tenant but also to sue him. Not only would he evict his tenant, but he would also take whatever possessions of value his tenant had. The disciple put his trust in the wrong place.

Where should the disciple put his trust? In the heavenly Father. He will take care of his children. He loves doing that, so the disciple should turn to God and ask him. He shares the disciple's values because they are his values. This perspective frees up disciples to live as Jesus has instructed them; in other words, to do to others as they would have others do to them. That pretty much sums up what Jesus called his disciples to do.

Can we think about how we may have judged others so that we feel better about ourselves? Can we recall times when we relied on people who did not understand kingdom values to help us in our struggles, only to find ourselves being used or hurt by those people? Both problems suffer from the same flaw: people wanting to be followers take their eyes off the Father and focus on people. That is never going to be a recipe for successful living as a disciple of Jesus. The road that Jesus walks is a tough road that no one, other than Jesus, walks perfectly. If we are going to walk a difficult road, it is necessary to keep our eyes on the one who walked it successfully and listen to his instructions on how to get down that road.

If you still have a pen and paper within reach, take a moment and write down some names. Write the names of people you have met and know who have helped you follow Jesus when it was not easy. They sounded like Jesus, and you saw them live out his teachings when it was not easy for them. They were so committed to Jesus that living counter-culturally was their nature, and they did it joyfully. This list can help you focus on spending time with the right people—people who can help you keep your eyes on Jesus on a difficult road.

Wrapping It All Up (7:13-27)

Jesus closes out his teachings with a reality check and a hard call followed by three illustrations. His hard call: diverge from the norm and go against culture. This call will inspire some, but most people will stick with the status quo, even if it kills them, and it will. Why? Because it is easier to go with the crowd, and more preferable than having the crowd turn on you. So Jesus basically informs his would-be followers that they will find themselves with few companions on this less-traveled road.

Then Jesus gave three illustrations to drive his message home: wolves in sheep's clothing; bad trees/good trees; a wise man/a foolish man. These illustrations are used by Jesus to drive home some truths. The wolves, the bad trees, and the foolish man will all end up in the same place. They will be rejected by Jesus because they did not do what Jesus taught. They may have heard his words and agreed, but they did not put them into practice. That can be recognized by all who see their lives; it surely would be recognized by Jesus.

However, those who heard Jesus' teachings and actually lived by them would be seen as true followers, and they would be received by Jesus. They also would find that their lives would withstand the storms of life because their lives were built on the rock-solid foundation of Jesus' teachings.

Where do we find ourselves in these illustrations? We are going to be found somewhere in them. We might fool ourselves into believing some wolf we listened to is actually a sheep, but Jesus will not be fooled. We might fool ourselves into thinking our religious fervor is all that Jesus is looking for, but Jesus will not be fooled. We might have a compelling list of reasons for why we did not actually do what Jesus taught, but Jesus will not be swayed by our list. Our lives will not hold up in the storms, and Jesus will tell us on that dreadful day of judgment, "Away from me, you evildoer. I don't know you." Won't those be terrible words to hear at that time?

However, we do not have to find ourselves in those parts of the illustrations. We can find ourselves as real sheep, and as good trees bearing good fruit, and as the wise man who built his house on the rock. We can do this by actually doing what Jesus teaches us to do. Right now, you have a whole block of teaching, the first in Matthew's gospel, to help guide you down the road of a disciple of Jesus.

Possibly you find yourself feeling overwhelmed by Jesus' teachings. Maybe you think that Jesus calls any would-be followers to walk an impossible road. And while it is true that most people will not choose to walk this road, there are many who do. They are an inspiring collection of people from all over the world, and remarkably, they are human beings with the same fears and flaws that you have. They are the people on your list, if you wrote one. They are the people on lists written by others. They are the people on Jesus' list, if he were to write one.

Two of the people on my list are a husband and wife. They had a good and comfortable life in a community where they could have lived out the rest of their days. They were surrounded by friends who were followers of Jesus. Life in the church they were connected to offered many blessings and advantages for them and their children. They chose a different direction, though, when the road they were on diverged and took them around a bend they could not see past. They felt led by Jesus to go to a place where the church was not strong, a place where they did not have a single friend who was a disciple. They felt led to be salt and light for the man's family and for others whom they would encounter. They paid a steep price on that road, but they also lived powerful lives that drew many to Jesus. They became Jesus' messengers to save others and help them find life. They are my parents, and they helped me understand the true glory and honor found on this road of following Jesus. They showed me that I can walk the road as well. In truth, many human beings show us this road can be successfully traveled.

Seat Belt Check

Did you find yourself overwhelmed by Jesus' teachings, or thinking there is no way you could live up to the calling of a disciple of Jesus? If that's what you're thinking, it's understandable. We struggle enough trying to imitate people we view as good role models; how could any of us imitate God? We may think that Jesus set the bar too high.

If we find within us the courage to at least try, how long do we imagine we will go before we fail, and fail miserably? How many times will we fail before we give up out of frustration? It might become more and more tempting to bail on Jesus with each failure. How do we stay buckled in?

I offer you two comforting and encouraging thoughts. You will need both if you are going to follow Jesus:

1) God provides extra-special help, out-of-this-world help, to all who choose to follow Jesus. When someone commits their life to Jesus in baptism, God moves into that person in the presence of His Holy Spirit (Acts 2:28; 1 Corinthians 3:16). The Spirit lives in them to transform them from the inside out (Galatians 5:22-25), helping them become more than they could be on their own and helping them break free from who they were (Galatians 5:19-21).

2) There are three texts that speak to how thoroughly and continually God's grace covers our failures as disciples (Romans 6; Hebrews 10:5-14; 1 John 1:5-10). God knew we could not be perfect as He is. He knew we would fail, over and over again. However, if we keep walking the

road of a follower of Jesus, He will make sure we do not get bounced off the road. He will keep cleansing us so that He sees us as perfect, even though we are not; and if He sees us as perfect, we are.

Are you encouraged to stay buckled in and keep following Jesus? I hope so. The tragedy is not when we fail; the tragedy is when we do not even get on the same road as Jesus. So hear Jesus and accept His call to walk a difficult road. He will help you succeed, and with His help, you will succeed.

Matthew 10
Second Block of Teaching

10 Jesus called his twelve disciples to him and gave them authority to drive out impure spirits and to heal every disease and sickness.

[2]These are the names of the twelve apostles: first, Simon (who is called Peter) and his brother Andrew; James, son of Zebedee, and his brother John; [3]Philip and Bartholomew; Thomas and Matthew the tax collector; James, son of Alphaeus, and Thaddeus; [4]Simon the Zealot and Judas Iscariot, who betrayed him.

[5]These twelve Jesus sent out with the following instructions: "Do not go among the Gentiles or enter any town of the Samaritans. [6]Go rather to the lost sheep of Israel. [7]As you go, proclaim this message: 'The kingdom of heaven is near.' [8]Heal the sick, raise the dead, cleanse those who have leprosy, drive out demons. Freely you have received; freely give.

[9]"Do not get any gold, or silver, or copper to take with you in your belts—[10]no bag for the journey, or extra shirt or sandals or a staff, for a worker is worth his keep. [11]Whatever town or village you enter, search for some worthy person and stay at their house until you leave. [12]As you enter the home, give it your greeting. [13]If the home is deserving, let your peace rest on it; if it is not, let your peace return to you. [14]If anyone will not welcome you or listen to your words, leave that home or town and shake the dust off your feet. [15]Truly I tell you, it will be more bearable for Sodom and Gomorrah on the day of judgment than for that town.

[16]"I am sending you out like sheep among wolves. Therefore, be as shrewd as snakes and as innocent as doves. [17]Be on your guard; you will be handed over to local councils and be flogged in the synagogues. [18]On my account, you will be brought before governors and kings as witnesses to them and to the Gentiles. [19]But do not worry about what to say or how to say it. At that time you will be given what to say, [20]for it will not be you speaking, but the Spirit of your Father speaking through you.

[21]"Brother will betray brother to death, and a father his child; children will rebel against their parents and have them put to death. [22]You will be hated by everyone because of me, but the one who stands firm to the end will be saved. [23]When you are persecuted in one place, flee to another. Truly I tell you, you will not finish going through the towns of Israel before the Son of Man comes.

[24]"The student is not above the teacher, nor a servant above the master. [25]It is enough for students to be like their teachers, and servants like their masters. If the head of the house has been called Beelzebul, how much more the members of his household!

[26]"So do not be afraid of them, for there is nothing concealed that will not be disclosed, or hidden that will not be made known. [27]What I tell you in the dark, speak in the daylight; what is whispered in your ear, proclaim from the roofs. [28]Do not be afraid of those who kill the body but cannot kill the soul. Rather, be afraid of the One who can destroy both soul and body in hell. [29]Are not two sparrows sold for a penny? Yet not one of them falls to the ground outside your Father's care. [30]And even

the very hairs of your head are all numbered. ³¹So do not be afraid; you are worth more than many sparrows.

³²"Whoever acknowledges me before others, I will also acknowledge before my Father in heaven. ³³But whoever disowns me before others, I will disown before my Father in heaven.

³⁴"Do not suppose that I have come to bring peace to the earth. I did not come to bring peace, but a sword. ³⁵For I have come to turn

'a man against his father,

a daughter against her mother,

a daughter-in-law against her mother-in-law—

36 a man's enemies will be the members of his own household.'

37"Anyone who loves their father or mother more than me is not worthy of me; anyone who loves their son or daughter more than me is not worthy of me. 38 Whoever does not take up their cross and follow me is not worthy of me. 39 Whoever finds their life will lose it, and whoever loses their life for my sake will find it.

40"Anyone who welcomes you welcomes me, and anyone who welcomes me welcomes the one who sent me. 41 Whoever welcomes a prophet as a prophet will receive a prophet's reward, and whoever welcomes a righteous person as a righteous person will receive a righteous person's reward. 42 And if anyone gives even a cup of cold water to one of these little ones who is my disciple, truly I tell you, that person will certainly not lose their reward.

Prepping for the Teaching

As you progress into Jesus' teachings, you sense that he is truly calling you into a different life. He is doing more than pulling you into some church worship service. You may be sensing that following Jesus down the same road he walked is going to turn your world upside down—all seven days of the week. Travel the road long enough, and you will learn that this road leads to a vastly superior life experience than what you could have found on any other road. As we enter into Jesus' second block of teachings, this is a truth you want to remember.

The setting for this block of teachings involves Jesus' preparation for sending his followers on a mission. He sends twelve men out with specific instructions about what he wants them to do, how to do it, what to expect, and how to respond. As we read these teachings and consider them, we need to do so with fresh eyes and ears. We are also sent out on a mission, down the same road, so we need to see what Jesus wants us to see and hear what he wants us to hear. We must set aside any predetermined ideas of what we believe is in these teachings, and we must set aside our reservations and fears. For now, we just listen to Jesus and allow his words to fill our minds and our hearts.

Before we delve into the actual teachings, it is worth noting the events that preceded the instructions. Jesus and his disciples had been traveling through Galilee, and Jesus was struck by two things: how much the people needed the message of the kingdom of heaven and how ready they were to hear it and respond to it. So he asked those following him to seek help from God to bring those people into the kingdom: *Ask the*

Father to send workers to bring in this harvest. I suppose those disciples started to pray for that. Then Jesus did something very unexpected; he chose twelve of their number to be his first workers, his first disciples. In essence, he told those twelve they were going to be God's first answer to the prayer. We should keep this in mind when we pray, for God may answer our prayer by using us as the initial answer. Be ready for that.

Now allow yourself enough time to read through the whole section of teaching in one sitting. Soak in every word and let those words wash over you. Let them sink in so that you feel their impact on your life. Take note of your feelings as these teachings sink in. Read the teachings as many times as you need. When you are ready, move forward.

The Thread That Does Not Run Through

As we move forward, we start by focusing not on what you read, but on what you did not read. You may have picked up on some threads of thought that ran all the way through Jesus' teachings. Let's take a moment, however, to note some threads you did not see: safety, security, protection from harm. For disciples in certain cultures today, this is unsettling, to say the least. These disciples have grown accustomed to such concepts being part of following Jesus. They have grown so accustomed to these elements being part of discipleship that any action that does not have these components automatically is replaced by a safe *Plan B.*

It has dawned on me that for many disciples in my culture, safety has become more than a desire—it has become a necessity. In truth, it has become more than a necessity; it has become a god. Safety dictates much of what many will do, or won't do. How many kingdom works have never been started because safety was not guaranteed? In my culture, hearts can be moved for great and important kingdom works to be done, but those same works can be radically altered or never even started because of fear.

I recall once preparing myself to take a trip to a part of the world that was not considered to be safe—the Texas/Mexico border. On the Mexico side, drug cartels operated without fear and without opposition. My desire was to go to the border and see firsthand the crisis swirling around undocumented immigrants crossing the border. I knew I needed to go further than Texas and actually cross into Mexico to see firsthand what was happening; I knew that would put me in a place where safety could not be guaranteed. This was also at a time when the border being closed was a real possibility. I could cross over and not be able to cross back.

As I made preparations for my trip, I asked the shepherds of my church to pray for me. They did, and one of the shepherds led that prayer. Two things still stick in my mind about his prayer: he prayed that I would not be put in danger; he prayed that I would not even have to cross the border on my trip. Guided by his reasoning, I would have never made the trip. After the prayer, I respectfully thanked the shepherd for his prayer, and I asked him to never say such a prayer for me again. I preferred that he pray for God to use me as he needed me to be used. That meant more to me than my personal safety.

The safe road is part of my culture, but it is not the way for many disciples in a large portion of this earth. Safety is not in their daily life, especially when they follow Jesus. Satan has many forces that he uses to try and silence followers of Jesus. Disciples in these places know that not only can they be persecuted, imprisoned indefinitely, or killed, but the same can happen to their families and anyone they love.

There is an incredible book that I have read multiple times, which I encourage you to read—*The Insanity of God* by Nik Ripken. It contains remarkable accounts of followers of Jesus in very dangerous places. Here is a comment by one disciple in Russia:

"For us, persecution is like the sun coming up in the east. It happens all the time. It's the way things are. There is nothing unusual or unexpected about it. Persecution for our faith has always been—and probably always will be—a normal part of life." (p. 161)

Keep these words in mind as you consider Jesus' teachings in this section. If safety has been part of your expectations and has shaped how you follow Jesus, you need to know that others are actually walking the scary and dangerous road that you read about in this section of Jesus' teachings. If other disciples can do it, so can you. We all can; we just need to keep our eyes on Jesus and trust him. More importantly, we need to decide what is more precious to us: our safety or following Jesus. The road we are on will not always take us to both. We must ask ourselves, *Where do we draw our line between following Jesus or being safe?*

Disciples Loved and Hated (10:5-15)

Jesus showed his followers where to draw the line when he sent out the first twelve to do two basic things: take care of the people's physical needs and pains, and proclaim a kingdom message. Picture in your mind the remarkable emotions those twelve felt when they heard Jesus' words. Jesus actually gave the disciples the power to do what he had been doing. They had watched Jesus heal many; they had heard him teach about the kingdom of heaven. This had to be stunning and exciting for them, as well as for the crowds. Who wouldn't want to be chosen by Jesus to do these things? They were about to become celebrities and sought-after heroes. Those twelve disciples had to be chomping at the bit, eager to bust out and do what they saw their teacher doing. They looked down this road and saw wonderful things happening.

Perhaps you can imagine what it felt like for those twelve disciples to witness firsthand the miracles Jesus did: to see blind people have their sight restored; to see lame people walking again; to see people set free from the torment of demons; or to see the dead raised back to life. Perhaps you can imagine how their blood pressure jumped with excitement and anticipation when Jesus told them about the authority and power he was giving them to do the same things. Maybe you can even visualize how each of these twelve men acted when they performed their first miracles.

You might even be able to imagine how the crowds responded when it was no longer just Jesus doing these things. If the crowds flocked to Jesus with their sick, diseased, possessed, and dying, would they not have done the same with these twelve men? Now they had options—six to be exact; they could go to any of six locations, wherever these pairs of disciples were, and get the healing and deliverance they needed. Now these twelve disciples were experiencing the same heady days they saw Jesus having. Those were good days to be disciples of Jesus.

If that was all Jesus had sent his first disciples to do, they would have become the most popular group in Israel. Everybody would have loved them; everybody would have received them. Who wouldn't welcome real, bona fide miracle workers? However, that is not all Jesus sent them to do. He also sent them out to proclaim the same message he was proclaiming—a message about the kingdom. While even that seemed exciting, Jesus knew something about the message and how it would affect people. His message would turn the discipleship road into a dangerous road.

Jesus knew that not everyone would welcome the message his disciples would proclaim; he knew they would reject not only the message but also the messengers. Not every town or home would roll out the welcome mat for his disciples. Likely, this was hard for those twelve disciples to grasp. How could someone receive a miracle of healing and then reject the message that came along with it? Jesus saw the paradox in the people's response and tried to prepare his disciples. Anyone who rejected this message would pay a heavy price, but so would his disciples. This reality would drive this block of teachings Jesus gave his disciples.

Before going further, we must consider these two elements of our mission: helping others with their needs and proclaiming the message of the kingdom. Do both aspects shape our road as we attempt to follow Jesus? Or do we choose one and let other people do the other part? Consider the choices you have been faced with and the choices you have made. If you choose one and not both, which one are you doing? Doing good works or proclaiming the kingdom message? Why did you choose only one, if that is what you did? If you have chosen to do only one, are you still walking the same road Jesus walked?

Let's reflect on this aspect of the road we walk. What is the focus of our mission? Do we see a desire to meet the physical needs of people? Do we see a desire to proclaim the message of the kingdom? Perhaps a pendulum best describes how disciples have often tried to follow Jesus. On one end of the pendulum is the disciple who is solely focused on proclaiming the message, paying little or no attention to the physical needs of the listeners. One of Jesus' first disciples, John, shot that approach down when he wrote to other disciples in his latter days— caring for physical needs was empty without a love that addressed those needs (1 John 3:16-18). To miss the needs or just respond with words alone is not the way of a disciple of Jesus. Thankfully, many disciples have moved away from this end of the pendulum swing.

On the other end of the pendulum swing are those disciples trying to follow Jesus who are heavily into good works that meet the physical needs of their listeners, but there is not much emphasis on proclaiming the message, if any. The rationale of these disciples is that people would rather see a sermon than hear one. Perhaps that is true, but Jesus knows they still need to hear the message. He sends his disciples out to proclaim that message, not just to do good works. Doing good works without proclaiming the message makes the disciples little more than a civic organization. Such discipleship loses what makes disciples of Jesus distinct—the teachings of their master.

Where are you in this pendulum swing? Are you at either extreme, or have you focused on both elements of the mission Jesus has given his disciples? Those who are on the extremes, whichever end, are not walking the same road as Jesus.

If you find yourself in a place where you have focused on doing good deeds and not proclaiming the message, you are in a particularly difficult place. When you go out to meet people in their pain and offer them relief from their struggles, maybe even deliverance, you find a receptive audience. You are their friend, even their hero, because nobody wants to stay in their pain. So whenever help comes that offers a way out, even if just briefly, the people in pain grab hold. They are happy, grateful, gracious, and respond with smiles and kind words.

Disciples can fall in love with being received as friends and heroes. So when they move from just good works that meet physical needs into proclaiming the message, they can find that the response quickly turns to respectful disinterest, dismissal, rejection, or even contempt. Disciples can find they are now regarded as a nuisance, as unkind or meddling, maybe even as an enemy. Would you go from being a hero to becoming an enemy in order to follow Jesus? That is a particularly difficult change of course for any potential disciple.

It would be so much easier, and more pleasant, if we could just be people who did good works to help meet people's physical needs, but that is not the road Jesus walked, or the road he sent his first disciples down. It is so important that we do not fail to follow Jesus in this aspect of our mission. Jesus never intended for his disciples to just focus on the physical. He would teach elsewhere that if a person saves their life but loses their soul, they have lost everything (Matthew 16:26). If disciples offer only help for people to save their physical lives, but offer no help for them to save their souls, what has really been offered? Jesus sends out his disciples, even today, for much more. This part of our mission makes us distinct, for we offer what no one else can. We must be willing to forego popularity and celebrity status so that we can give people the message that addresses their spiritual needs.

Down the Dangerous Road (10:16-25)

Let's zoom in with our microscope and look closer at this mission. Jesus sent his first disciples on a mission that he knew would lead to rejection. What did that road of rejection look like? In his teachings, Jesus pulled no punches and used no subtleties to soften the reality that would hit his disciples. Jesus probably said much more than those twelve men wanted to hear, but he wanted them to know it all so that they could be prepared when it happened. As you listen to Jesus' teachings, commit to staying buckled in and not bailing. You surely will not feel anything different from what those first twelve disciples felt when they heard these teachings for the first time. Most of them stuck with Jesus—all except Judas—and so can you.

Jesus informed his disciples that rejection would come in many forms—all scary, all difficult, many painful, some deadly. They would be arrested and jailed. They would be put on trial. They would be betrayed by close relations, even their closest family members. They would be persecuted, flogged with whips, hated by all, even killed for proclaiming their teacher's message. They would be viewed as the devil by many.

Before they walked this dangerous road, though, they would watch their teacher and master walk it first. They would see him walk the road before them, and they would know they were truly walking in his footsteps. In so doing, they would be doing no more than him, suffering no more than him. They would know they were doing what was expected and that they were living up to their calling as Jesus' followers. Perhaps Jesus hoped that this would be enough for any would-be follower to travel this dangerous road.

I recall stories of people going into battle, people who knew they were likely to die in the battle. Even if they were uncertain of their fate, they knew they were about to enter into a conflict too terrifying to think about, but they had to. They had to prepare themselves to see the battle all the way through—to whatever end. I suppose each person had to look deep inside to see if they believed their mission was worth whatever price they had to pay.

So Jesus pulled the curtains back on the real plot that unfolds in this world every day. He showed his followers the conflict between the forces of good and evil, the conflict between two kingdoms that were diametrically opposed in goals and values. Consider this: whether you choose to follow Jesus or not, the conflict goes on. If you choose to follow Jesus, you get to be part of the forces of good for a better outcome for all you hold dear. If you have to pay the ultimate price for those people, would it be worth it?

Let us not fall into the fatalistic thinking that Jesus sends his followers out on suicide missions, though. Nor does he send them to defeat. Neither of these possibilities has a positive outcome. The mission of Jesus has a very positive outcome. With fresh ears, let us hear Jesus' instructions to his followers who walk this dangerous road.

In 10:16-17, Jesus instructed his followers to be as shrewd as snakes and to be on their guard. When walking this dangerous road, it would be wise to keep their eyes open and their wits about them. They would not be walking among people who had their best interests in mind. Jesus did not expect his disciples to be reckless and bring trouble upon themselves that was not necessary. When you read Ripken's book, *The Insanity of God*, or the companion book, *The Insanity of Obedience*, you will notice that some modern-day disciples have learned this lesson.

These instructions did not mean the disciples were able to get off this dangerous road or that persecution would not happen if they were guarded and used their wits. Quite the contrary, Jesus said the arrests, floggings, trials, and dying would still come. However, he did tell them they would get help. What help did he promise? They would not have to worry about what to say because the Spirit of the Father would help them give witness by giving them the very words to say (10:19-20). What

Jesus made evident to those twelve men was that their physical safety was not the ultimate concern; rather, it was the mission of proclaiming his message. Jesus sent his disciples into harm's way to get his message out.

It was not as if Jesus had no concern for his disciples' physical safety. He loved them, so how could he not be concerned? He knew they did not want to suffer and die, just as he would not when he faced his own death. That is human nature. He referenced those human survival instincts in 10:23 when he spoke about fleeing persecution. And yet, even when fleeing danger, they must not lose their mission or purpose; they must keep witnessing.

If you read Acts 8, you will find this scenario unfolded when the disciples faced persecution in Jerusalem. They fled Jerusalem, but they did not hide. That persecution became the tool Jesus used to send his disciples to new places. They carried out their mission, and the message never stopped being proclaimed; as a result, more people came into the kingdom, and they became proclaiming disciples. In modern times, in places of the world where followers of Jesus are persecuted, many disciples keep proclaiming the message of the kingdom. The result? The kingdom grows.

Let's look further at ourselves. How and where do you see the message of the kingdom being proclaimed? Have you seen disciples put themselves in harm's way in order to proclaim the kingdom message? If so, you probably were inspired and energized by their example. If all you have witnessed, though, are disciples doing what they can do in safety, you are feeling a different energy when you read these teachings of Jesus. This is a deadening and strangling energy. If that is you, fight for a new vision and see the lives of disciples who walk the dangerous road. Be awakened by the life and energy on that road.

I know a disciple, an older woman, who found her mission unfold after her community had been devastated by a hurricane. She would travel twenty miles one way in an unreliable car to load up food and printed Bible messages. Then she would travel thirty miles into hard-hit areas, searching out people who needed those supplies.

She gave these strangers the supplies that were loaded in her car, including the Bible messages. She prayed over those strangers and encouraged them to seek God. Many times she would be in these places and her car would break down. She would have to call her son to come get her. However, she did not know where she was, and he had to find ways to track her down. Did that stop her? No. The next week, she would do the same thing again.

I know disciples who are used to living where drug cartels operate in a country that is not safe on any given day. One particular family is a husband, wife, and two small, precious children. He is a preacher, and he and his family lived in a house on the same lot as their church building. One night, they were awakened by the sounds of racing engines, screeching brakes, and automatic gunfire outside their house. The police had chased cartel members to the intersection where their house was located. That is where the shootout occurred. This did not prompt the couple to pack up and move away to a safe location. Actually, they were in the process of building a new house in a nearby neighborhood. Was it safer there? No. The cartel operated out of a house at the end of that block. In fact, the preacher was informed that while his house was being built, cartel members were going into it at night to use the electrical outlets to recharge their phones. When I asked the husband and wife, a father and a mother, if they were concerned about the safety of their children with all the violence around them, I encountered the same attitude and faith that I read about in those disciples in Russia. Danger was part of their world, part of their lives, and they were staying so that they could be God's messengers to those people.

I know a follower of Jesus who was applying for citizenship in my country. He was on the brink of being granted that privilege when he felt God prompting him to stay in his home country and carry out his mission there. When he was called before the judge who was ready to give him citizenship, he respectfully declined. Needless to say, the judge was shocked and could not believe this disciple was throwing away his golden opportunity. This follower left this country, left his wife, and went back to his home country. He bought a garbage dump in the middle of a cartel-infested community and built a shelter for immigrants. That mission is blessed by God today as he takes care of physical needs and proclaims the kingdom message to all. The shelter is walled in, but the cartel not only leaves his work alone, they even provide protection. Not too far into his walk on this dangerous road, his wife gave up her citizenship in this country and joined him. They have no regrets and live with joy and purpose as they follow Jesus wherever he leads them.

Perhaps the road of following Jesus has not gotten dangerous for you yet. If not, Jesus' teachings in Matthew 10 can overwhelm you. You were glad to become a disciple when you knew it meant salvation for your soul. You were glad to be part of a church where the worship thrilled and energized you and the people loved you. You couldn't wait to join in the good works of helping others. You heard messages about the danger of being a disciple in some parts of the world, but that was not you, and you never considered it would be. You were content to pray for those in danger as you carried on your good works in relative safety. What will you do, though, when the road you are on turns dangerous? What message will you speak then? You should consider that; this could be the first step that keeps you from bailing on Jesus. As you consider this, though, be sure to give weight to the joy and purpose that elevate life into the realm of the divine. That kind of life is only found on this road. What a shame it would be to miss out on the divine because of too much concern for acceptance and safety.

Jesus Has His Disciples' Back (10:26-33)

If God is love, and if he is powerful and in charge, and if Jesus is King of kings, we might wonder why followers of Jesus even have to suffer. Why do the Father and Son not just protect them and keep them safe from all harm? If people are willing to walk the dangerous road of a disciple, will Jesus not have their back? The answer to that question is a resounding, Yes! However, this does not remove the disciples from physical danger or harm. Instead, Jesus' teachings expand the vision and understanding of his disciples so they can see a bigger picture and have a fuller understanding of safety.

Jesus did not expect his disciples to be without fear when they followed him down this dangerous road of proclaiming the kingdom to a broken and lost world. He knew fear would never be far away. So Jesus told them what should really bring fear to their hearts, and it was not having people kill their physical bodies. Rather, what should really terrify them is that the Father in heaven could become so angry with them that he would not only kill their bodies but send their souls to hell to be destroyed. Jesus said it was better to have people, instead of God, as an enemy.

Perhaps this does not give you much comfort as you think about this part of Jesus' teachings. So let's spend some time here and go deeper. You noticed that Jesus started this part of his teachings with the thought that there wasn't anything concealed that would not be disclosed. Disclosed to whom? That would be the Father. Who would do the disclosing? That would be Jesus (10:32-33). When Jesus reveals to his Father the identities and actions of those who are killing his disciples, what do you suppose the Father will do? They will be some of the people the Father destroys in hell, body and soul. The enemies of Jesus' disciples may have thought they were all-powerful and answerable to none. They were completely mistaken, for when they persecuted Jesus' disciples they made the worst enemy possible: the Father in heaven. Their day of reckoning would come upon them terribly.

Give some thought to the disciples who were persecuted and killed by those enemies of Jesus. What will happen to them? Did Jesus deliver them from persecution and death? He told those first twelve that they were precious to him and the Father; even the hairs on each disciple's head were known by the Father and Son. They were definitely known and loved by both Father and Son, so Jesus reassured them and told them not to be afraid. However, he did not say he would deliver them from physical persecution and death. He promised something far greater: if they would still follow him and acknowledge him as Lord when they faced that persecution, even if it was death, he would stand up for them before the Father in heaven. They would have no need to fear that the Father would destroy them; rather, he would gladly and lovingly welcome them. That is how Jesus had the backs of his disciples.

On the other hand, if any disciple denied Jesus in the face of persecution and death, Jesus would deny them before the Father. What would be the fate of those disciples? They would face a fate worse than death, just like their persecutors. Their souls would be destroyed in hell. Jesus would stand tall for the disciples who stuck to him on the dangerous road; the disciples who bailed on him would not have such an advocate, and they would have much more to fear than physical pain and death.

Through the centuries that have passed since Jesus ascended to heaven, his disciples have traveled this dangerous road of discipleship. Countless have suffered and even died. Whole families of disciples have died for their Lord and Teacher. The enemy of all of Jesus' followers, Satan, has exacted a terrible price from so many. He believes that many will deny Jesus if he makes the price too high. There have been those who did not want to pay that price and who have turned away from following Jesus. They bailed and saved their skins for the moment, but they entered into a dark place where they will face the Father's judgment without the Son's advocacy. If they turn back to Jesus and follow him, they can still change their fate; if not, they face a terrible fate. Not all have turned away from Jesus when the price got too high. They pay the price, and they will be welcomed into eternity with glory and honor.

Disciples join a war when they become followers of Jesus; they do not just join churches with exciting programs. They become warriors in a war for what is good and holy. Winning this war has cost the Father and the Son greatly, something we remember every year around Easter and every time we share in the meal we call the Lord's Supper. Like any war, many combatants will suffer and die. Those combatants are often the disciples of Jesus; however, they do not suffer and die in vain. They meet their fate with great hope and assurance. Why? They know their Teacher has their back where it counts the most.

There is an aspect to this suffering and dying that is an amazing twist. One would think that Satan would be celebrating whenever a disciple of Jesus dies; after all, that means one less warrior for the Lord on the battlefield. Yet, that has not been how the war has unfolded. Look at history, and you will see that when a disciple dies for Jesus, the number of disciples has often grown. How is that possible? Those who once belonged to the enemy are often convicted by the disciples' faith as they suffer and die. They become convinced that Jesus must really be Lord and King, and they switch allegiance. Jesus' army grows, the devil's army gets smaller. Satan cannot win even when it looks like he is winning. This has got to be maddeningly frustrating to him. He must know he is doomed and that he will lose this war.

Perhaps you have known all of this before reading this book; or perhaps, you never thought of it and no one ever told you. Knowing what you are engaged in makes a huge difference. Church membership is probably not worth dying for, at least in the way we often think about churches that meet in buildings. However, when we know that any suffering and dying we may face contributes to something worthy, we can find the will, the courage, and the faith to make that sacrifice when it is required of us. We can live small or live large in this life; Jesus gives us the opportunity to live large.

What Matters Most to a Disciple (10:34-39)

People who fear conflict want peace. People tired of conflict want peace. People who have never known conflict want peace. Peace is a sweet idea, but it has so often eluded our grasp. If peace is desired so much, why is it so elusive? Why did the angels proclaim peace on earth when Jesus was born, and why, in this block of teaching, does Jesus proclaim he did not come to bring peace? When it comes to peace, we find there is a difference between intent and reality. We cannot fault God or Jesus when reality does not live up to their intent. Instead, we find that people are the problem, and have been since the days of Cain and Abel. Some people just don't want to do what is needed to have peace.

If Jesus was intended to be the source of peace, then peace only comes when people listen to him and follow his teachings. Peace will continue to elude those who refuse to listen to him: nations, social groups, families, and individuals. As long as people continue to follow self-seeking desires instead of following Jesus' teachings of love and holiness, peace will remain an unrealized dream.

The refusal of many to follow Jesus also impacts those who are his followers. Just as those people opposed Jesus, even violently, they have also opposed his disciples, even violently. Those first disciples found that opposition would arise within their own family relationships. Perhaps this was not the case with the first twelve, but it would be with others who followed Jesus. Peace that once had been in their homes would be lost because of Jesus. Jesus would end up bringing a sword into their lives. This did not happen because Jesus wanted it to; it happened because people would hate his teachings so much that they would hate his disciples, even if it was a family member.

Jesus spoke of this earlier in his teachings (10:21); now he picks that thread up again and confronts his disciples with a terrible decision. For many, the day would come when they would have to decide who was more important to them, who they loved more. Would their answer be Jesus? Or a family member such as a father, mother, or child? Family members turning on disciples may have seemed unthinkable to those first disciples. How could someone who loved them and raised them turn on them? Or how could someone they had loved and raised turn on them? What was unimaginable to those disciples would become a reality for many. Their pain and suffering would run deeper because of the source; and in that pain, they would have to make a choice no one should ever have to make.

How could Jesus make such a choice requisite to following him? To follow him, disciples had to keep moving in the same direction toward the Father. This road is non-negotiable for it is the only way to the Father. This is another reason why Jesus' teachings were so important. They provided guidance in times when followers were conflicted at the deepest level. When pressure to bail on Jesus came from a parent, child, or other family member, the disciple would be torn between two foundational allegiances. Where did their heart lie, and what relationship was really important to the disciple? This is an unfair choice, but Satan specializes in putting disciples of Jesus in such binds. He believes that the price is so high that many disciples will bail on Jesus if they have to make this choice. Through the ages, he has put followers in this heart-wrenching bind.

Many who would follow Jesus today are still put under the same pressure. Years ago, I met a pre-teen girl. She was twelve when she committed her life to Jesus through her baptism. This did not sit well with her family. Her parents and grandparents told her that she had one month to turn away from her commitment to Jesus. If she did not turn away from following Jesus, they would throw her out of their house and out of their family. That was a huge load of pressure to put on one so young.

Perhaps most of us cannot fathom how we would respond if that same choice had been put on us at the same age. Where would we go? How would we live? How would we get by without the only family we had known? Twelve-year-old children cannot get jobs and leases on apartments. Maybe many of us would engage in creative thinking and reasoning to forego such a choice. Not this young girl. She did not turn away from God when that month had passed; and she was thrown out. Other disciples took her in and loved her. She had a new family when she lost her birth family. One of the blessings of the Lord's church is that it becomes a network of supportive relationships when it is functioning as Jesus intended. Love can be found in that group when it cannot be found elsewhere. Love can cross every social barrier so that all can be welcomed into new homes and families.

The call to follow Jesus will require change from all who answer the call because the discipleship road is also a holy road. All who walk it go through change. Yet, it does not matter where one comes from or what one has done; all are welcome and all are called. To be received in love when making such life changes is an awesome blessing. This love can fill a disciple, and thankfully so. However, disciples of Jesus must not forget that even though the church loves them and supports them, their culture will not. They have made a choice to go counter-culture, and they will become outsiders, outcasts, and even enemies. When the disciple's family chooses to stay in the culture, the disciple will have a terrible but necessary choice to make that will reveal where their heart truly lies.

The pressure to choose between family and Jesus is terrible enough, but it could be worse, and has been worse for many disciples. Sometimes they have had to choose between living or dying, and the determining factor for their fate would be their commitment to Jesus or their denial of him. Of those first twelve disciples, all would have to make that choice. One chose not to follow Jesus and to turn on him. His reward? Thirty pieces of silver. His fate? He could not live with what he had done to Jesus and the choice he had made, so he took his life. What happened to the other eleven? Like so many others, they were killed because they followed Jesus. What mattered most to them? It was not keeping their life here and losing their life with the Father. They knew that was the better option.

What did those disciples understand that we need to understand today? How is it possible to be so in love with Jesus that we would give up everything for him, even our very lives? What kept them buckled in when they wanted to bail? If we can find that same understanding, we can make the same difficult choice if it comes our way. We will think more about this in our next seat belt check, but ponder over this until then. Perhaps now is a good time to spend some time in prayer. Maybe you need guidance. Maybe you need your fears to be calmed so that your heart can slow down. Maybe you know you will need courage you have not witnessed in yourself. Pray for what you need, even if you do not know exactly what you need.

Easing the Road for His Disciples (10:40-42)

Jesus closes out his second block of teaching with a teaching about welcoming and then seals that with three illustrations (much like the first block). You recall Jesus spoke earlier in his teachings about how his disciples would be received by the people in the towns and cities. Sometimes his disciples would be welcomed, sometimes not. His disciples would face much hatred, suffering, persecution, and even death; however, Jesus included a final thought that could lessen their danger and hardship on this dangerous road.

Jesus made some promises his disciples could lean on, and he preceded these promises with a clear view of who was behind his disciples. The person who welcomed one of his disciples into their home was actually welcoming Jesus, the teacher of those disciples. Not only were they welcoming Jesus, they were welcoming the Father in heaven into their home. That reality gave Jesus' disciples greater standing. They would be no mere mortals because they represented the Divine and the Holy. The person who was considering the choice of welcoming or rejecting Jesus' disciples was now informed as to who was coming into their homes, and it would not be just people.

Rejection and mistreatment of these representatives would bring judgment from the Father (10:15, 28). These followers had an advocate and they had recourse. They could shake the dust off their feet (10:14) and withhold peace from that town or home (10:13). These were not symbolic and empty gestures; they were appeals to the Father in heaven to bring judgment upon those homes and towns.

Welcoming those disciples would bring reward. The Father would notice, and just as he would reward the disciples of Jesus who went out as prophets and righteous people, he would reward those who welcomed Jesus' messengers. Those hosts and recipients would also be blessed. Jesus knew those hosts would be putting themselves in danger also, and he promised to reward them just as he promised his disciples. Jesus went on to teach that even the smallest kindness shown to one of his disciples, just giving them a cold cup of water, would not go unrewarded by him. Even though these people were not present to hear these teachings since Jesus only had his disciples as an initial audience, we know those twelve shared these promises with those they encountered on their mission. In fact, Matthew made sure they knew by writing it down to be read.

Does this last part of Jesus' teachings bear true for Jesus' disciples today? Do disciples who go out today still stand as representatives of Jesus and the Father? Do disciples still have the power to call on the Father and the Son to stand up for them? Will the Father and Son still bring judgment or reward to people based on whether they receive the messengers Jesus has sent out? There is no reason to assume either the Father or Son has changed, or that they fail to take notice; so there is no reason to assume they will not act on behalf of these modern disciples.

What does this second block of teaching mean for you, someone who wants to follow Jesus? There are some of Jesus' teachings that grab your attention more than others. I will not go over those again, but I will offer you a perspective that is revealed in these teachings. You are offered an opportunity to live your life on a mission that brings you into the realm of the Divine and Holy. This dangerous road is a sacred road. Expect not just fearful things; expect wondrous things as well.

Seat Belt Check

Why would a disciple follow Jesus if the road they walk is so dangerous? As those first disciples considered going on the mission their teacher was sending them on, certainly they considered this question. Throughout Jesus' teachings in this section, there were insights about danger and greater danger, rewards and greater rewards. What they heard was that no matter what choice a person made regarding following Jesus, life would be filled with pain and reward. Those first disciples could weigh out which choice was preferable.

Imagine this scenario: a person is told they can choose between dying from a wasting, painful disease, or they could choose to die a quick death by drowning. If you could ask that person which means of death they would prefer, that person might despairingly respond, *"What's the difference?"* There is no real choice because neither suffering has an upside. There is just suffering that leads to death, and there is no greater purpose to lift the suffering out of being more than just suffering.

What happens when something elevates the suffering? Imagine a scenario where a father sees his small child being swept away in a flood. He can watch his child be swept away, knowing his child will drown. Or he can jump in to save his child. If the father cannot swim, what will he do? Will he sacrifice his life to save his child? Or imagine a father escaping a burning house, only to hear his child screaming, who was accidentally left behind in the house. What will the father do? Most fathers will instinctively sacrifice their lives if there is the remotest chance they can save their children. They gladly choose suffering and dying if there is a higher purpose. This is a remarkable quality of humanity. People will go through great pain and suffering when they know it is for a higher purpose.

Another human quality also lifts us up above just being creatures. We want our lives to matter. Nobody likes to have a meaningless life or a meaningless death. Young people dream of making the world a better place. Older people never really lose that dream. Maybe it gets reshaped, but it is not lost. That is why people volunteer, why they go to poorer countries and give up part of their lives to help strangers. When people get the opportunity to live large rather than live small, they usually choose large. If they believe in the purpose, they will jettison comfort and safety and sacrifice. A higher purpose and our innate desire bond and enable us to do what we did not know we could do.

If Jesus' teachings in this second section are so tough that you want to bail, think long and hard about this: there really is no choice about whether or not you will suffer and die. Both lots come to all people. What matters is what will your suffering and dying count for? The disciples of Jesus who suffer and die for him will always come out winners.

So for what will you suffer and die? Make sure it is for a purpose that will give meaning to your suffering and dying. Make your living and your dying count for as much as possible.

Matthew 13

Third Block of Teaching

13 That same day, Jesus went out of the house and sat by the lake. [2]Such large crowds gathered around him that he got into a boat and sat in it, while all the people stood on the shore. [3]Then he told them many things in parables, saying: "A farmer went out to sow his seed. [4]As he was scattering the seed, some fell along the path, and the birds came and ate it up. [5]Some fell on rocky places, where it did not have much soil. It sprang up quickly because the soil was shallow. [6]But when the sun came up, the plants were scorched, and they withered because they had no root. [7]Other seed fell among thorns, which grew up and choked the plants. [8]Still other seed fell on good soil, where it produced a crop—a hundred, sixty, or thirty times what was sown. [9]Whoever has ears, let them hear."

[10]The disciples came to him and asked, "Why do you speak to the people in parables?"

[11]He replied, "Because the knowledge of the secrets of the kingdom of heaven has been given to you, but not to them. [12]Whoever has will be given more, and they will have an abundance. Whoever does not have, even what they have will be taken from them. [13]This is why I speak to them in parables:

"Though seeing, they do not see; Though hearing, they do not hear or understand."

[14]In them is fulfilled the prophecy of Isaiah:

"You will be ever hearing but never understanding;

you will be ever seeing but never perceiving.

[15]For this people's heart has become calloused;

they hardly hear with their ears, and they have closed their eyes.

Otherwise, they might see with their eyes,

hear with their ears, understand with their hearts and turn,

and I would heal them." [1]

[6]But blessed are your eyes because they see, and your ears because they hear. [17]For truly I tell you, many prophets and righteous people longed to see what you see but did not see it, and to hear what you hear but did not hear it.

[18]"Listen then to what the parable of the sower means: [19]When anyone hears the message about the kingdom and does not understand it, the evil one comes and snatches away what was sown in their heart. This is the seed sown along the path. [20]The seed falling on rocky ground refers to someone who hears the word and at once receives it with joy. [21]But since they have no root, they last only a short time. When trouble or persecution comes because of the word, they quickly fall away. [22]The seed falling among the thorns refers to someone who hears the word, but the worries of this life and the deceitfulness of wealth choke the word, making it unfruitful. [23]But the seed falling on good soil refers to someone who hears the word and understands it. This is the one who produces a crop, yielding a hundred, sixty, or thirty times what was sown."

[24]Jesus told them another parable: "The kingdom of heaven is like a man who sowed good seed in his field. [25]But while everyone was

sleeping, his enemy came and sowed weeds among the wheat, and went away. ²⁶When the wheat sprouted and formed heads, then the weeds also appeared.

₂₇The owner's servants came to him and said, 'Sir, didn't you sow good seed in your field? Where then did the weeds come from?'

²⁸'An enemy did this,' he replied.

"The servants asked him, 'Do you want us to go and pull them up?'

²⁹" 'No,' he answered, 'because while you are pulling the weeds, you may uproot the wheat with them. ³⁰Let both grow together until the harvest. At that time, I will tell the harvesters: First collect the weeds and tie them in bundles to be burned; then gather the wheat and bring it into my barn.' "

³¹He told them another parable: "The kingdom of heaven is like a mustard seed, which a man took and planted in his field. ³²Though it is the smallest of all seeds, yet when it grows, it is the largest of garden plants and becomes a tree, so that the birds come and perch in its branches."

³³He told them still another parable: "The kingdom of heaven is like yeast that a woman took and mixed into about sixty pounds of flour until it worked all through the dough."

³⁴Jesus spoke all these things to the crowds in parables; he did not say anything to them without using a parable. ³⁵So was fulfilled what was spoken through the prophet:

"I will open my mouth in parables, I will utter things hidden since the creation of the world."

[36]Then he left the crowd and went into the house. His disciples came to him and said, "Explain to us the parable of the weeds in the field."

[37]He answered, "The one who sowed the good seed is the Son of Man. [38]The field is the world, and the good seed stands for the people of the kingdom. The weeds are the people of the evil one, [39]and the enemy who sows them is the devil. The harvest is the end of the age, and the harvesters are angels.

[40]"As the weeds are pulled up and burned in the fire, so it will be at the end of the age. [41]The Son of Man will send out his angels, and they will weed out of his kingdom everything that causes sin and all who do evil. [42]They will throw them into the blazing furnace, where there will be weeping and gnashing of teeth. [43]Then the righteous will shine like the sun in the kingdom of their Father. Whoever has ears, let them hear.

[44]"The kingdom of heaven is like treasure hidden in a field. When a man found it, he hid it again, and then in his joy went and sold all he had and bought that field.

[45]"Again, the kingdom of heaven is like a merchant looking for fine pearls. [46]When he found one of great value, he went away and sold everything he had and bought it.

[47]"Once again, the kingdom of heaven is like a net that was let down into the lake and caught all kinds of fish. [48]When it was full, the fishermen pulled it up on the shore. Then they sat down and collected

the good fish in baskets, but threw the bad away. [49]This is how it will be at the end of the age. The angels will come and separate the wicked from the righteous and throw them into the blazing furnace, where there will be weeping and gnashing of teeth.

[50]"Have you understood all these things?" Jesus asked.

[51]"Yes," they replied.

[52]He said to them, "Therefore every teacher of the law who has become a disciple in the kingdom of heaven is like the owner of a house who brings out of his storeroom new treasures as well as old."

Prepping for the Teaching

The third block of Jesus' teachings about following him contains a series of parables. There are two audiences that Jesus speaks to in this block: the crowds and his disciples. It is clear that Jesus' primary focus is on his disciples, for it is to them that he explains his parables. Jesus does not explain his teachings to the crowds, not because he does not care about them, but because he is focused on training his disciples. Those disciples will be the ones he sends out to teach the crowds so that they can understand and choose to follow him as well.

As you have done with the first two blocks of teachings, take time to read this third block. Read it several times if you need to. Try to find the thread that runs through the teachings. When you are ready, we will take a closer look at these teachings to see what is there for us to learn and to apply as we walk the road of a disciple of Jesus. We can expect to learn new things about following Jesus down this narrow road that most will not take. We can expect to be challenged; perhaps we will find these teachings are also frightening. Hopefully, we are growing through our frightening moments so that our thoughts move towards understanding and following better, and not towards bailing. We will still do a seat belt check when we work through these teachings though. We don't want to lose anybody along the way.

The Thread That Runs Through

You noticed certain dynamics as you read this third block of teaching. The teachings center around two groups of parables Jesus taught. What separates them is Jesus changing locations from the boat to the house. Included in that is a change of audience; the larger crowd is not present for the last group of parables. In the first group, Jesus had to explain two parables to his disciples. The first parable is explained to his disciples after they seemed to have pulled him aside to ask a question; the second was not explained until they were back in the house. There is also the element of Jesus' teachings being hidden, even taken, from some people while others are given the opportunity to receive.

These dynamics reveal a thread that runs through these teachings. We need to spend some time with this thread if the parables are going to impact us as much as Jesus intends. For starters, consider that you are going to be in one of two groups: the one where you are given the knowledge of the secrets of the kingdom of heaven, or the one where whatever knowledge you have is taken away. We will take a look at that first audience who heard these teachings so that we can compare that with the current audience who reads them. There are obvious implications and consequences that follow for every listener and reader, depending upon what group they are in. To see this thread, we will first look outside the parables in the teachings and notice what is happening there. That draws our focus to 13:10-18, 13:34-35, and 13:51-52.

13:10-18

In the preceding verses, it has been revealed by Matthew that Jesus had already begun teaching the crowds about the kingdom. However, this was different from the teachings Jesus gave on the mountain in Matthew 5-7. In this teaching, Jesus used a story or parable to convey his message. A parable could be confusing and its meaning uncertain. If that was the case, how could the people learn the message Jesus was teaching? Because of that, the disciples pulled Jesus aside and asked him why he was teaching in such a way.

Jesus' response to his twelve disciples draws us into our thread: there are people who have eyes and ears to see and hear, and there are people who do not. You noticed that in the two parables Jesus had to explain to his twelve, he added the statement, *"Whoever has ears, let them hear."* Once he said that at the end of telling the parable, and once he said it at the end of explaining the parable. Jesus knew that even though he could say the same thing to everybody, not everybody would hear him. Not everybody wanted to hear and understand him. In some people, Jesus was hindered by a stone wall of already made-up minds.

People in that mental place were not open to learning new things, discarding old thoughts and ways that needed to be discarded, or changing their minds. When Jesus quoted the prophet Isaiah, he referenced a statement about people who hardly hear with their ears and who have already closed their eyes. They were people who had calloused and hardened hearts. If they were willing to change and be open to him, Jesus could help them discover the kingdom, but he could not teach them if they were not open to him.

What distinguished the twelve disciples of Jesus from that other group was not their keen intellect and sharp minds. Sometimes those twelve men could be pretty dense and pretty slow to understand, but they were open and willing. They were teachable. They would eventually grasp his teachings, sometimes more quickly than other times. They were becoming disciples of Jesus. So Jesus spent extra time with them, explaining what they did not initially understand. You noticed that happened a couple of times in this third block of teaching. The twelve had some knowledge of the secrets of the kingdom of heaven, and Jesus was giving them more.

If the twelve disciples were in that group of receiving, who was in the group of losing what they had? We get an answer to that when we go back to Jesus' first block of teaching and see his indictment of the Pharisees and teachers of the law. These religious leaders of the people had been entrusted by the Father to teach the people correctly about the kingdom. They were doing very badly at that; in fact, they had failed. Jesus spent much of his time trying to guide people beyond the teachings of these religious leaders. His efforts to do that would make Jesus the enemy of those men. You will notice this if you read all of Matthew's gospel at some point. This conflict would come to a boiling point. In Matthew 23, Jesus publicly scorched the Pharisees and teachers of the law for their hypocrisy and failure to teach about the kingdom. In Matthew 26, those religious leaders would conspire and have Jesus executed. So it would be safe to say that Jesus had those people in mind when he spoke of some losing what they had been given. Their eyes, ears, and hearts were closed to Jesus' teachings, and he could not penetrate that hardness.

We cannot limit that second group to just those religious leaders though. Many in the crowds would be included in that group as well. Jesus was speaking to them in parables too. Why would their eyes, ears, and hearts be closed to Jesus if they were coming to listen to him? Perhaps they were only coming for the miracles. Perhaps they were open to teachings that made them feel good and comforted them. Perhaps they were the kind of people who would compare Jesus' teachings with their local religious leader, their synagogue rabbi, but would choose the teachings of their rabbi over Jesus at the end of the day. Whatever their reasons were, Jesus knew their hearts. Until their hearts changed and they became open to following his teachings, they would lose what had been given to them, their standing as kingdom people.

13:34-35

As Jesus closed his teaching in parables to the crowds and moved back into the house, Matthew emphasized that Jesus had deliberately chosen to use parables to speak to these people of closed ears, minds, and hearts. What he had made available to them in parable form were secrets of the kingdom, teachings that held truths never revealed before. They were hearing from the Son of God himself, and yet, they would miss out. This was the danger of having already made-up minds. It would cost those people dearly.

13:51-52

Jesus closed out his teachings with some questions for his twelve disciples and a cryptic statement. He had taken extra time to help the twelve understand some parables they struggled with initially. Now at the end, he wanted to make sure they understood all he had just said. They answered in the affirmative, and Jesus accepted their assessment of their understanding.

Then Jesus said something cryptic to close out his teachings; if you take a moment to look closer, you will likely be scratching your head in puzzlement:

"Therefore, every teacher of the law who has become a discile in the kingdom of heaven is like the owner of a house who brings out of his storeroom new treasures as well as old." (Matthew 13:52)

Did Jesus just say something positive about the teachers of the law? If so, this is the only place in any of the four gospels where Jesus had something positive to say about that group. There was one teacher of the law that Jesus commended (Mark 12:28-34); however, Jesus never spoke positively about the whole group, particularly in Matthew's gospel. We should conclude, then, that Jesus is not referring to that group in this positive statement.

Who is Jesus speaking of, then? Remember our thread. There was the group who was being given the secrets of the kingdom of heaven, his disciples. They were being given more, while the Pharisees and teachers of the law were losing what they had been given. Those twelve disciples would be Jesus' teachers of the law. Any who had ears to hear and understand him, and eyes to see and perceive him, and hearts that turned to him became his teachers of the law. They would be the ones he would give his message to so that they could teach others what he had taught them.

The thread that runs through this teaching is that Jesus was looking for a new group of people who could carry his message about the kingdom to others. He could not work with the established religious leaders, so he was raising up his own disciples, people who could be taught something new. He would equip them to pass along the treasures of the kingdom. Some would be old treasures they had already known, and some would be new to their experience.

These disciples would become valuable messengers for their teacher and to the people. That would be a very high purpose and calling for those twelve men, as it is for any follower of Jesus. A word of warning though: just as Jesus took away what had been given to the Pharisees and teachers of the law, he can do the same with other teachers of the law who fail to hear him, see him, turn to him, and follow him. That would include us.

Now it is time to consider how this thread applies to us. We find ourselves in similar places, do we not? We have our religious heritages and traditions, and our religious leaders. We might be third, fourth, or fifth-generation Christians. One consequence of such a heritage is that we bring our own preconceived religious ideas into the reading of Jesus' teachings. That does not mean something sinister is lurking in our hearts; sometimes it just means we have blind spots that rob us of understanding.

Once I was helping a man read the Bible for the first time in his life. He had tried reading Genesis and struggled mightily through the whole endeavor. When he finished Genesis, he was frustrated that he had not understood much. I suggested he try reading Matthew, which he graciously and eagerly accepted.

Every week, I would touch base with him and ask how his reading was going. He was excited and would share with me what he had read and understood. At some point, I would pass along some small bit of insight to enrich his reading and understanding. Then he would go home and read for another week.

Soon he came to the last chapters of Matthew, the place in the story where Jesus was arrested, beaten, and crucified. When I saw him next after he read those chapters, I asked him how his reading had gone. I expected the same eager, energetic response; however, what he said shocked me and caught me completely off guard. He confessed that he was not able to read those chapters. I was at a loss as to what to say, so I asked him why he couldn't. He replied that as he was reading, he was getting angry and actually started to weep. He was upset that the people were treating Jesus so horribly when he, above all people, did not deserve any of that.

I was stunned and speechless at first. This man who was reading the Bible for the first time understood this part of it far better than me, someone who had grown up hearing and reading the same story. I never, in all my reading, got angry when I read the end of Matthew. I never shed even one tear. As much as I appreciated my upbringing, and I would never trade it in, I realized I had lost something as a result. It took a man reading the story for the first time to help me realize that. Perhaps this story helps you understand how your great inheritance of generational faith has probably robbed you as well.

Sometimes heritage and preconceptions are not so benign. They can be so strong in us that our minds are already made up when they should not be; we know what we believe, and we are not open to change. While we may have been students with a willingness to learn at some earlier point in our lives, we may have lost that. When we read Jesus' teachings, they are filtered through our preconceptions, and everything offensive to us is washed out or diluted. If that is happening, we resist listening to Jesus. If we hear some message that does not align with what we learned from our grandparents or parents, we resist it. We might even try to get the messenger removed. What is Jesus to do with us then? Can he break down the stone wall of our *set-in-stone ideas*? Jesus' teachings cannot reach us if we have lost our willingness to see, hear, turn, and change.

If we look deeper into our attitudes and ways, we come to another problem: a condescending attitude. We judge the original crowds harshly because they had Jesus speaking directly to them, and yet so many of them chose to listen to their religious leaders. It seems a lot of Christians have the same problem today. They join a church because they like the preacher. When that preacher moves on, so do they. If that preacher retires, and the new preacher's sermons don't grab them, the crowds move on. Jesus did not move on or retire, but somehow that one preacher became the only one people wanted to listen to. They could not hear Jesus through the next preacher. This is an all-too-real trap for preachers and crowds.

Perhaps that is a trap that ensnares televangelists and megachurches. Religious leaders, even those leaders who are trying to follow Jesus, want a following. They hone their skills and techniques, and even their message, to draw as many people as they can; and there are many who will be drawn. These preachers are clever and crafty, funny and engaging. They are the highlight of every service, for the people usually rate the service by how good the sermon was. If these messengers are effective, they can build a large following, which becomes a large church. That usually leads to big buildings and big budgets. It then becomes important to *feed the beast* so that the people keep coming and the infrastructure and salaries can be paid. The preacher has to keep drawing the crowds.

This desired result leads to an undesirable consequence. The need to keep drawing a crowd can put pressure on the messenger, the message, and the crowds. If the messenger walks the same road Jesus walked, then unpopularity inevitably comes into play, because much of Jesus' message is unpopular. Will the messenger follow Jesus when the message is unpopular, or adapt to the crowd in order to keep drawing them? Will the crowds still listen to the messenger when it gets hard and unpopular, or will they move on to another preacher who is popular somewhere else and noted for his comforting sermons? Sadly, some messengers and crowds end up on a different road than Jesus at such times.

Perhaps we have some planks to remove from our eyes so that we can really see Jesus. Perhaps we need to unstop our ears by clearing out some voices that have hindered our hearing so that we can really hear Jesus. Perhaps we need to rediscover how to be students again, learning new things that make us uneasy alongside the old things that we need to hang on to. We have an opportunity to receive great treasures from Jesus, and with that, a great mission. We also have the ability to lose it all by shutting Jesus outside of our stone walls. We need to find out who we are really listening to. This is the thread that speaks to us now.

The Parable of the Sower (13:3-9, 18-23)

Having laid the groundwork, we now turn to the first parable Jesus gave in this block of teachings. It was about a farmer sowing seed that landed in four different types of soil. Some who have studied this parable like to call it the parable of the soils. That is understandable since the soil makes all the difference in the results. Yet, Jesus referred to this as the parable of the sower, placing more emphasis on the sower. We will look at the soil, but we will try to keep the emphasis where Jesus placed it.

The sower is not identified in the parable, but considering the teachings that are given throughout this section, we can easily identify the sower. Initially, it is Jesus. Later it is his disciples. Jesus is setting realistic expectations for his disciples when they go out with his teachings. They should not expect the majority of people they teach to become disciples.

Understanding the types of soil would help his disciples understand the reactions they would encounter on their road. No matter how clearly they spoke the teachings of Jesus, there would be people with hard hearts, and they just would not understand the message or be able to receive it. This sounds similar to the thread we identified, doesn't it? The disciples would encounter the same stone walls that Jesus did. The result would be that Satan would be able to quickly remove the teaching before it could take root.

The second soil would be particularly disheartening to the disciples when they encountered it. They would teach the message of the kingdom to some people who would quickly and joyously receive it. They would be like a flash fire, quickly flaring up, but just as quickly going out. They would follow the teachings as long as it did not cost them anything, but if being a follower of Jesus caused any pain or discomfort, they would bail.

The third soil represented people who liked the message of the kingdom, but they would not let go of their desire for money or their worries about how to get by or get ahead. Do you remember the teachings of Jesus in the first section? Rich and poor alike would have a hard time choosing God's righteousness over concerns related to money. The disciples would find that people they taught would struggle with the same issue.

The fourth soil stood for people who actually became disciples. They would hear and understand. Then they would teach others and help extend the reach of the kingdom. These people had ears to hear, and the harvest they would bring about would be a great encouragement to the disciples who taught them.

Jesus laid out for his twelve followers a clear view, an accurate lay of the land. They would experience a harvest, but they would also experience failure and heartbreak that went hand in hand with the joy of the harvest. They would pour out sweat, blood, and tears to bring people into the kingdom. Sometimes it would seem like they had pitifully little to show for all their efforts and sacrifices; and sometimes, they would be shocked where the harvest actually occurred.

I am drawn to a memory of a young couple I met when I was starting out as a preacher. I was working with a church that had gone through great trials and had lost many of its members. It was struggling to survive when I arrived. I was truly clueless about how to help, but sometimes the Lord blesses the ignorant, and good things happen. This couple lived in the apartment just across the church's parking lot. Both the husband and wife were open to hearing the message. The wife was eager to receive the message and was soon baptized. Not too long after that, the husband was also baptized. Prior to hearing the message of the kingdom, both had been drug users, and the wife's brain had been badly and irreversibly damaged by the drugs. By age, she was an adult, but she had the emotional and intellectual level of a teenager. The husband had not suffered such damage, and he wanted to learn everything he could about God and the kingdom. When I saw him, however, I was disappointed. He had so much to learn, so far to go, before he could be of any use in that struggling church.

I confess, I prayed to God about him. In my prayer, I said something like, "Lord, I asked for your help in raising up spiritual leaders for this church. I am thankful for this new brother, but he is not a leader." It was a pretty ignorant prayer. In the next year, I saw this young disciple throw himself fully into the work of the kingdom. In an incredibly short time, he was growing into a spiritual leader. By the end of the year, I was celebrating how God had brought us the leader we needed. Then the young man informed me that he was moving away for a better-paying job that would allow him to support his family better. Then I found myself mourning the loss of a leader we needed. I found myself complaining to God in my next prayers about bringing us a great leader and then letting him move away. It was another ignorant prayer. Little did I know who God was bringing us next.

We never know where the harvest is going to come from, especially when we experience times when there is no harvest. If you have been a teacher for Jesus and have sown the seed of the kingdom, you may have gotten discouraged at some point because it seemed like there was no harvest. Maybe that prompted you to focus more on good works than teaching because you knew people would accept your good works and accept you. It is hard to face rejection, but that is often the life of a disciple of Jesus, going through one disappointing experience after another. However, when the harvest does come and the sower experiences that, there is no comparable joy in this world. Even in our disappointment, we can find strength and comfort knowing we are in the middle of God's will because we are walking the same road that our teacher walked. Remember who you are and what you have been called to do. You are Jesus' new teachers of his law. Hold your head high, keep your eyes on your Lord, and let your mouth speak freely and often about the teachings he has given you.

The Weeds and the Field (13:24-30, 36-43)

What is the kingdom of heaven like? Each of these remaining parables of Jesus gives some insight into this. Some are fairly simple in structure and contain a single insight; however, the one about the weeds in the field has numerous elements, and the disciples needed help understanding it. Jesus told the parable when he was with his disciples and the crowds; the explanation occurred in private after Jesus had gone back to the house. What Jesus told those twelve still gives understanding for all today who would be his followers. Our attention now turns to the parable of the weeds and the field.

When you read the parable, did you consider it to be a parable about wheat or weeds? We might have thought it was about wheat since that was what the owner planted. However, the twelve picked up on the weeds, and they asked Jesus to explain to them the parable about the weeds in the field (13:36). Like the servants in the story, the weeds drew their focus. Why? Because the weeds presented problems. They weren't supposed to be there. Perhaps the disciples picked up on the idea that the weeds would present problems to them when they were out spreading Jesus' teachings. So let's keep our focus on the weeds as we work through the parable.

As the first disciples heard this parable and its explanation, one thing they learned right away was that the kingdom of heaven is present on this earth. That was clear when Jesus told them the field was the world. When the disciples went out to spread the word about the kingdom, they would not be solely focused on what would happen in the age to come; their message was relevant for life in this world.

Other elements in this story involve the two main powers in the story: the owner and his enemy. The owner had the power and opportunity to plant wheat; the enemy had the power and opportunity to plant weeds. The sowing of weeds reveals something about the enemy— he wanted to ruin the efforts of the owner. The presence of weeds would choke out and diminish the crop that was planted. That was the intent of the enemy. As expected, the intent of the owner was to have a bumper crop, as much as possible. Jesus identified the owner as himself. He identified the enemy as the devil.

This parable unveiled a setting of conflict between the two, a conflict the twelve would unavoidably step into. The scale of the conflict had to be more than they had considered. In their Jewish heritage, they accepted that the Messiah would lead the Jewish nation in a successful revolt against their enemy—the Roman Empire. Jesus taught them something different: instead of leading people in rebellion against Rome, they would be part of a force that was directly taking on the devil. That was a battle and conflict of a much higher magnitude.

The wheat gives us insight into Jesus' intent for the kingdom. The wheat was good, and so Jesus intended his kingdom to be good. Yet, his kingdom would not be untouchable. It could be damaged and diminished by the devil, at least temporarily. The devil's effort to sow weeds throughout the field of wheat was his effort to do just that.

In the parable, the owner's servants were significant to the story, but they were not identified by Jesus. We might understand them to be Jesus' followers, perhaps correctly; however, Jesus identified his followers in the story as the wheat. Maybe the followers of Jesus made up both groups. Those first twelve followers would have definitely been the wheat, as would any followers afterward. The wheat had one role in the story—to be harvested. The servants helped plant the wheat and expected their role would be to get rid of any weeds. They found out that was not their role, though, for that role belonged to the harvesters. When the parable moved into the struggle between weeds and wheat and the harvest to come, the servants moved out of the story as the harvesters moved into it.

The counterparts of the wheat were the weeds, the followers of Satan. They not only were in the world, but they were mixed in with the followers of Jesus. Jesus told his disciples a terrifying truth about the weeds: they looked like the wheat. In other words, it could be hard to distinguish between a follower of Jesus and a child of the devil. This was not because they did the same things; rather, Satan is pretty good at camouflage. Later, at another time and in another writing (2 Corinthians 11:13-15), Paul (one of Jesus' followers) wrote to some other followers who faced some big problems. Those churches, which were one part of the kingdom of heaven, were having internal problems, and the source of the problems was the children of the devil. They were masquerading as children of righteousness, as part of the church. Satan and his children are good at disguising themselves, mixing among the righteous, and causing problems. This is what Jesus told his first followers to expect when he explained this parable to them.

The solution was not for the workers to pull all of the weeds but to let the owner send out harvesters, those who could recognize who truly was wheat and who really were weeds. The harvest element of the parable pronounced who was the real power in the story—it was Jesus and not the devil. Jesus would send out angels to weed out his kingdom. Those angels would gather up all who did evil and caused evil and throw them into the blazing fires of hell where they would meet their judgment.

This solution was a lot to take in for Jesus' disciples. Those twelve were being told that their work in the kingdom was going to be difficult because Satan would put his people in the way to oppose them, and he would attempt to undo their efforts in order to limit their effect. That probably would not have thrilled the twelve followers because nobody wants to constantly deal with the biggest and baddest bully on the block. That, however, was part and parcel of their mission of being Jesus' followers and teachers.

The encouraging part of Jesus' explanation, though, was hearing that Jesus and his angels were on their side. Jesus would eventually and ultimately get rid of the weeds. When that happened, at the end of the age, then the wheat would really shine and be blessed. The harvest time was going to be a great time for the wheat. It would mean an end to the never-ending struggle with Satan and his followers. It would mean no more fighting evil or the temptation to give in to evil. It would mean no more fighting to survive and remain a child of righteousness. For them, the harvest time was something to look forward to.

The harvest would not be a good time for the devil and his children, though. Those who had lived as weeds and caused so much trouble in this age would not see the next, at least not the good part of it. The prospect of blazing fire and weeping and gnashing of teeth does not give comfort to those who will meet such a fate; instead, it brings terror to them when they recognize what awaits them.

This parable would become part of the teachings the disciples would tell others. They would share a message of conflict, both internal and external. They would proclaim a message of endurance in the midst of struggles, of fighting temptations to do evil. Their message would proclaim only two possible outcomes: deliverance for some and destruction for others.

As we compare ourselves with those first followers through the lens of this parable, what do we notice? What do we learn? Is there anything new for us to take in? I believe that just as the parable has many elements, there are a number of insights and takeaways for us today.

For those who see following Jesus in such a way that they can get along with the culture or try to win it over by bending to it, I believe they will experience only frustration, futility, and a sense of betrayal. Satan only acts like he wants to get along, as do his children; but their goal never changes, for they seek to destroy any harvest Jesus might get. When children of righteousness try to get along with a culture that is filled with the weeds of the devil, they will find the weeds will turn on them and betray them as their real purpose comes to the forefront. It is impossible to be in step with people going in a different direction, one that has a purpose that is the polar opposite of Jesus'. Jesus' earlier teachings about being as shrewd as snakes and innocent as doves might be echoing in your ears right about now.

Another insight centers around followers of Jesus who have assumed an ability that Jesus said they cannot have. They want to be the owner's servants and claim the role of harvesters. They are quick to identify those they claim are not in the kingdom. They might be right sometimes, but they will not always be right. The result will be that they will pull up a child of righteousness and destroy that person because they identified him or her as a child of the devil. Jesus told his disciples to leave that job up to the angels he will send out on the day of harvesting and judgment. In the story, he denied the servants the role of harvesters, so we know he denies it to any who serve him today.

There was a time when I would have been among those who thought they could identify who was saved and who was lost, who was being righteous and who was being evil. I am thankful I learned this element of the parable because it kept me from doing great harm. Just one example would be the time I met a certain man who lived with a woman he would not marry. I believed that was clearly evil, and I still believe it usually is because of certain biblical teachings. I have seen Satan do great harm to people with the lie that getting married is not necessary. One day, however, I met a man and woman of whom I was not so sure.

They were an older couple who lived in poverty in a run-down house behind a bar. The woman had lived most of her life with paranoid schizophrenia. When she was on her medications, she could function normally. However, one of the complications with this disease is that people with it do not feel they need the medication when they are on it. When on the medication, they feel good, and they are functioning normally. The result is that many stop taking their medications; soon afterward, they struggle again under the terrible effects of the disease. That was the cycle this woman continually went through. She had two adult children, a son and daughter, who finally got so tired of their mom's cycle, they wrote her off and refused to even associate with her. They were tired of being called in the middle of the night because their mom was walking down the street in some dangerous neighborhood in her nightgown. So they washed their hands of their mom and exited from her life.

There was this older man who loved this woman. He did not want to see her harmed. He was willing to take her in and care for her, and love her. He would try to help her stay on her medication, and he would be there to protect her when she was off. The problem he faced was that her medication was very expensive, as well as very necessary. His work insurance would not cover her medication if they were not married, and not even if they did get married because of the cost. However, her insurance did cover the cost of the medication, but she would lose her insurance if she married this man. What should he do in this dilemma? He did the only thing he knew to do: he let her move in with him without getting married so that he could take care of her. He would be as a husband to her, and she as a wife to him, but they could not marry.

When I met this man and woman and learned their story, I knew I had no alternatives for them. I also knew I did not have the ability to discern if he was doing evil or good. I knew that my role was to help these two people in any way I could, as little as that help might be, and to let Jesus and his angels make the call on who this man and woman were. I would not be the least surprised or disappointed if Jesus' angels determine them to be wheat and bring them in with the rest of the harvest.

There is another insight about this parable that I share with you. There is surely more to learn, but I will limit myself to one more. I live in a culture where there is no longer a belief in judgment, an event where there will be a separation of the evil from the righteous, where the righteous will live forever, and where the evil will be thrown into the fires of hell and destroyed. I notice that in my culture, everyone is going to heaven, and they go straight to heaven when they die. It does not matter how a person lived or what they believed or who they followed. Everybody gets a ticket punched for heaven when they die. I have seen papers run artists' images of some famous person who just died, and the image has them walking through the pearly gates of heaven, complete with angel wings and halos. I have also been to funerals of believers, people I sincerely believe to be righteous. At these funerals, I have heard preachers proclaim that the person is already in heaven, chatting it up with their loved ones who have been waiting in heaven for them since their deaths. These are surely comforting images to us, but they are not the images that Jesus drew in any of his teachings, certainly not here. For some reason, we have dismissed Jesus' teachings about a judgment day.

Perhaps we have bent to our culture, not just with the imagery, but also with the message. We preach on love, and rightly so. However, when we focus so much on love that we throw out judgment for evil, we are not right. We profess to be followers and messengers of Jesus and his teachings. So if Jesus spoke often of judgment, we have lost that part of our teaching. We need to start listening to Jesus again. We need to figure out how to speak about Jesus' love and Jesus' judgment. Both are real, and the latter is not dispensable just because we are uncomfortable with it. It is part of the message people still need to hear.

When Jesus sends countless people he loved to the blazing fires of hell, will he have something to say to followers who kept silent about that judgment and did not warn those people? If Jesus looks his followers in the eye after pronouncing that terrible judgment, what will his disciples see? Maybe some of those could be saved from judgment if we have the courage to speak about it. Would that not be real love on our part?

The Mustard Seed and the Yeast (13:31-33)

The remaining two parables Jesus spoke before leaving the crowds drove home the same point: his kingdom was going to grow exponentially bigger than anyone then could imagine. Jesus was starting something, and it was only in its infancy. Just like a tiny newborn baby, his movement looked small to all who were watching. Observers from the ruling culture were checking out his movement, but it likely seemed insignificant to them. After all, they had the establishment, the synagogues, and the temple; they had a host of religious leaders embedded in society. What did Jesus have? He didn't even have a house, and he had twelve unimpressive men who were following his teachings. Jesus and his followers might cause trouble for the establishment, but they would only be a temporary nuisance.

No doubt those first twelve disciples felt small at times, like when they went into towns and cities in pairs, having to depend on strangers' hospitality, preaching their message on the streets and in the fields instead of the synagogues. They had not been selected to be disciples of the established rabbis and had gone into lesser professions, so they would not have automatically been given respect and honor by the people. As they listened to their teacher, they probably had their own doubts about how effective they would be, especially when Jesus was telling them they were going up against the devil and his forces.

The timing of these two parables was excellent. It gave those twelve disciples a look into what was going to come. They were helping their teacher start something that could not be stopped; it would grow into a movement bigger than any of them could envision. They were not building a synagogue where only a limited number of people would meet; they were building a kingdom that would draw people from everywhere. At this point, they did not know who would come or from where they would come, but their teacher was telling them it was going to be huge. These parables had to be a boost of confidence for them, as they should have been. They were the beginning of something very special.

Thousands of years later, we have witnessed how this kingdom has spread all around the globe. Yet, even we do not know how big it is, for there are places where disciples are not counted because they are being persecuted. There are no church rolls in such places. Those in power in those countries do not want word getting out about the growth of Jesus' kingdom there, but still, information and stories leak out. This kingdom continues to grow exponentially, and only the Father, Son, and Spirit know the real size of it.

This is an encouraging thought for disciples of Jesus today, for we can still feel small and insignificant. Sometimes we wonder if we are making a difference. The news we hear usually just reports the evil that happens around us, seemingly everywhere around us. If the news reports on any spiritual occurrence, it is often dismissive, derogatory, or scandalized. So there are times when the followers of Jesus need a reality check, when they need to be reminded that they are part of something that is growing exponentially still. Every follower of Jesus who carries out his or her mission on this road of discipleship is contributing to that growth.

There was a particular summer when I was struck by how awesome this kingdom is and how unstoppable it is. I was part of the staff at a week-long Bible camp for high school students. There wasn't a large number of students present at that session. Not even all the cabins were filled. Maybe there were fifty to sixty students at that session. Initially, it seemed quite underwhelming to me. Then the Lord got my attention; I started thinking harder about what was happening. Fifty to sixty teenagers had given up eight days of their lives, setting aside summer jobs, social media, and their normal circle of friends. For those eight days, they were spending two hours every day studying the Bible, several hours in different types of worship, spending their free time talking about spiritual things, loving one another, and being loved. They were praying and singing with passion numerous times every day. Several would surrender and commit their lives to following Jesus through their baptisms. They were building up spiritual strength to go out and fight the devil and his forces when they left the camp. What an awesome reality I was witnessing!

Then my understanding got even better. I started to think about other camps, camps all over the country and all over the world. How many teenagers were in those camp sessions? Like the session I was in, those took place every year. Added to that were the other camp sessions for younger ages. The scope of just these summer Bible camps was staggering. It did not even take into account the other works of disciples with other people in their societies. When I thought about all of this, I realized that there was no way the devil could stop the kingdom. He did not then, and does not now, have enough power, resources, or control to do that.

So when you head out to do your part in kingdom work and kingdom teaching, take a moment to understand what you are part of. You are involved in something huge that is getting even bigger. What you are doing as a follower of Jesus is significant, and you are significant. Don't let anyone tell you otherwise, not even yourself.

The Treasure and the Pearl (13:44-46)

We need to understand the setting and the mood in the room when Jesus told his twelve followers these two parables. Imagine you were one of those twelve. Jesus had just explained the parable of the weeds in the field. What a sobering reality for those followers to embrace. When they had decided to follow Jesus, they had imagined they would be taking on the forces of Rome; they could not have conceived they would be taking on Satan and his hordes. They had seen enough people terrorized by demons to know Satan was scary. Do you imagine any of those twelve were having second thoughts about following Jesus? Would you have?

Again, Jesus' timing for these parables is impeccable. When you look at those twelve, consider what they had given up to follow Jesus for a lengthy period of time, a period of time that was still ongoing. Their lives and their lifestyles had been turned upside down. Now they were being told that it would get harder and costlier. Were they at a point where they decided the sacrifices outweighed the benefits?

The two parables Jesus told stressed something that Jesus knew his followers did not yet fully know: the kingdom of heaven was such a valuable treasure that it would be worth everything a person gave up for it. There was no way those twelve could really grasp that truth, but they needed to hear it and trust that their teacher was telling them the truth. They needed to be reassured.

Perhaps you are in such a place as you follow Jesus. You may be carrying incredible wounds and scars that were inflicted on you by the devil and his forces, perhaps even literally. Maybe you have paid a great price in broken or lost relationships. Perhaps you have lost your livelihood because you chose to follow Jesus and his teachings instead of conducting yourself by the standards of your surrounding culture. Perhaps people have ridiculed or mistreated you because you were speaking the teachings of Jesus to them. Today you know you are hurting. As you look down the road, you see more pain coming your way, perhaps even worse pain. Your teacher is telling you that the kingdom is worth all of that and even more. You can't really know that, so you just have to trust your teacher is telling you the truth. He has been honest and straightforward with you from the start. Do you trust him, even with your life? He hopes you will, and he is counting on you, just like you are counting on him.

The Net and the Fish (13:47-50)

When Jesus closed out his third block of teaching, he closed with a parable that held imagery those twelve men were familiar with, especially four or five of them. It was a fishing parable. Around the Sea of Galilee, everybody would have seen with their own eyes how the fisherman separated the good fish from the bad. Several of the men Jesus called to follow him were fishermen; they had done their own separating of bad fish from the good, throwing away the bad fish and keeping the good. They had mental memories and muscle memories of doing that separation.

In the prior parables, Jesus had given positive reasons to the twelve men to keep following him in spite of the difficulties and dangers ahead of them—the kingdom of heaven is of far greater value than anything else in their lives. They should not lose such a treasure when it was offered to them. In this last parable, Jesus offered a compelling reason to follow him by going to the other end of the spectrum—avoid the blazing fire where there will be weeping and gnashing of teeth. Treasure or fire? It was their choice.

Jesus knew both possibilities needed to be heard by those twelve men. If they were to follow him down that dangerous road of discipleship, those twelve men needed to know what was at stake. They would not be striving for some gold-embossed star they could lick and stick on a performance chart. Their reward was a far greater treasure. Failure to follow Jesus would not result in a time-out in the corner of their room; far worse, their judgment would be harsh, terrible, and unthinkable.

There was no offer their enemy, the devil, could make to those twelve men that would be greater than what Jesus offered in the kingdom of heaven. There was no pain the devil could inflict on them that would be worse than what their Father in heaven could mete out, which was the destruction of their souls. These parables were a bottom-line kind of moment for those twelve men. When they tallied up the pros and cons of following Jesus, what was the bottom line, and which was the better choice for those twelve men? Eleven of them would understand the truth of what Jesus taught, and they would follow him all the way to their deaths. They knew what they wanted and what they did not want.

Now we think about us. What would motivate us to walk the dangerous road of following Jesus? Do we not respond to both rewards and punishment, carrots and sticks? Sure we do. At every age of our lives, both have been used by those who were trying to get us to do something that we needed to do. We needed both the carrots and the stick. Sometimes the carrots didn't work, and some stick was needed. Sometimes it was the other way around. That is our nature, so Jesus lets us know both options are on the table.

Whether we like it or not, we need to hear both options. As disciples, these options can keep us from bailing on Jesus. For those we call to follow Jesus, the presentation of these two options may be enlightening to them because it may be the first time they were told the gravity of their decision. With this information, they can make the best choice, even if it is a hard choice. Jesus did not overplay one option and downplay the other. He spoke plainly and pulled no punches with his followers. We owe the same to those we call to follow Jesus.

Did those twelve men understand what Jesus was telling them? They said they did. Do you understand what Jesus is telling you? Do you have a better grasp of what it means to follow Jesus after going through three blocks of specific teachings from Jesus about just that? Perhaps you began this examination of his teachings with competing emotions of fear and exhilaration; hopefully, they work together and grow into resolution. If you are hearing Jesus, you can find yourself being steeled for the journey that is before you. Even though you cannot see around the next bend, you know that whatever is there, you will not be put off. You know you will follow Jesus, and he is worth everything you have to go through. You know you are on a mission that is far bigger than Sunday church attendance, and you are ready to live large. You know that you cannot walk this road alone, but Jesus has walked it before you, and he walks with you. Why? Because he is your teacher, and you are his follower; on this road, that is what the teacher and his followers do—they walk the difficult road together.

Seat Belt Check

There are numerous versions of this poem circulating. It seems Mary Louis Stevenson was the author of the original. This one is a bit different, but perhaps it will serve you well enough as a seat belt check at this time. Perhaps, at some point, it will keep you on the road that Jesus has called you to travel.

Footprints in the Sand

One night I dreamed a dream.

As I was walking along the beach with my Lord,

Across the dark sky flashed scenes from my life.

For each scene, I noticed two sets of footprints in the sand,

One belonging to me and one to my Lord.

After the last scene of my life flashed before me,

I looked back at the footprints in the sand.

I noticed that at many times along the path of my life,

Especially at the very lowest and saddest times,

There was only one set of footprints.

This really troubled me, so I asked the Lord about it.

"Lord, you said once I decided to follow you,

You'd walk with me all the way.

But I noticed that during the saddest and most troublesome times of my life,

There was only one set of footprints.

I don't understand why, when I needed you the most, you would leave me."

He whispered, "My precious child, I love you and will never leave you,

Never, ever, during your trials and testings.

When you saw only one set of footprints,

It was then that I carried you."

Matthew 18
Fourth Block of Teaching

18 At that time the disciples came to Jesus and asked, "Who, then, is the greatest in the kingdom of heaven?"

[2]He called a little child to him and placed the child among them. [3]And he said: "Truly I tell you, unless you change and become like little children, you will never enter the kingdom of heaven. [4]Therefore, whoever takes the lowly position of this child is the greatest in the kingdom of heaven. [5]And whoever welcomes one such child in my name welcomes me.

[6]"If anyone causes one of these little ones—those who believe in me—to stumble, it would be better for them to have a large millstone hung around their neck and to be drowned in the depths of the sea. [7]Woe to the world because of the things that cause people to stumble! Such things must come, but woe to the person through whom they come! [8]If your hand or foot causes you to stumble, cut it off and throw it away. It is better for you to enter life maimed or crippled than to have two hands or two feet and be thrown into eternal fire. [9]And if your eye causes you to stumble, gouge it out and throw it away. It is better for you to enter life with one eye than to have two eyes and be thrown into the fire of hell.

[10]"See to it that you do not despise one of these little ones. For I tell you that their angels in heaven always see the face of my Father in heaven.[11]

[12]"What do you think? If a man owns a hundred sheep and one of them wanders away, will he not leave the ninety-nine on the hills and go to look for the one that wandered off? [13]And if he finds it, truly I tell you, he is happier over that one sheep than about the ninety-nine that did not wander off. [14]In the same way, your Father in heaven is not willing that any of these little ones should perish.

[15]"If your brother or sister sins, go and point out their fault, just between the two of you. If they listen to you, you have won them over. [16]But if they will not listen, take one or two others along, so that 'every matter may be established by the testimony of two or three witnesses.' [17]If they still refuse to listen, tell it to the church; and if they refuse to listen even to the church, treat them as you would a pagan or a tax collector.

[18]"Truly I tell you, whatever you bind on earth will be bound in heaven, and whatever you loose on earth will be loosed in heaven.

[19]"Again, truly I tell you that if two of you on earth agree about anything they ask for, it will be done for them by my Father in heaven. [20]For where two or three come together in my name, there am I with them."

[21]Then Peter came to Jesus and asked, "Lord, how many times should I forgive my brother or sister who sins against me? Up to seven times?"

[22]Jesus answered, "I tell you, not seven times, but seventy-seven times.

²³"Therefore, the kingdom of heaven is like a king who wanted to settle accounts with his servants. ²⁴As he began the settlement, a man who owed him ten thousand bags of gold was brought to him. ²⁵Since he was not able to pay, the master ordered that he and his wife and his children and all that he had be sold to repay the debt.

²⁶"At this, the servant fell on his knees before him. 'Be patient with me,' he begged, 'and I will pay back everything.' ²⁷The servant's master took pity on him, canceled the debt, and let him go.

²⁸"But when that servant went out, he found one of his fellow servants who owed him a hundred silver coins. He grabbed him and began to choke him. 'Pay back what you owe me!' he demanded.

²⁹"His fellow servant fell to his knees and begged him, 'Be patient with me, and I will pay it back.'

³⁰"But he refused. Instead, he went off and had the man thrown into prison until he could pay the debt. ³¹When the other servants saw what had happened, they were outraged and went and told their master everything that had happened.

³²"Then the master called the servant in. 'You wicked servant,' he said, 'I canceled all that debt of yours because you begged me to. ³³Shouldn't you have had mercy on your fellow servant just as I had on you?' ³⁴In his anger, his master handed him over to the jailers to be tortured until he should pay back all he owed.

³⁵"This is how my heavenly Father will treat each of you unless you forgive your brother or sister from your heart."

Prepping for the Teaching

We start into this fourth block of teaching as we have with the first three. Take whatever amount of time you need to read it, as many times as necessary, to become familiar with the teachings. Take some notes about what stands out to you as you read the teachings. Note any questions that come to mind as well. Perhaps we share some of the same thoughts. Whenever you are ready, we can move forward. We are in no rush, and we want to become familiar enough with the teachings that we can build understanding into them.

The Thread That Runs Through

As you search for this thread, you may struggle to find it. The first part of Jesus' teaching has a definite focus on children. The second part of his teachings is focused on forgiving people who don't deserve forgiveness. What possible thread is connecting the two parts? I suggest to you that the thread running through this fourth block of teaching is understanding who is worthy of honor in the kingdom of heaven. In a worldly culture, the person worthy of honor is lifted up and welcomed, but the person deemed unworthy is counted as irrelevant and disposable. Let's see if this possible thread runs true in the text.

Who might those twelve men consider to be unworthy of honor, irrelevant, or disposable? Children might be one group of such people. In that Jewish culture, children did not hold positions of honor. These twelve men were chosen by Jesus, handpicked by him, to be his teachers and help him build a kingdom. They would be the type of people who would be honored. Kingdom building was pretty important work, and these men took their roles in that work seriously. However, when they answered Jesus' call to follow, they brought some baggage with them: their cultural mindset.

When you live in a culture, it is often hard to identify where that culture has shaped you. These twelve men had no less of a problem with that than we do. They were blind to the fact that they carried their culture into their understanding of how to follow Jesus when it came to honor. Like their culture, these twelve men hungered for honor. The pursuit of honor was the province of men in their culture. Little children were not central to that pursuit. What time do important men have for children when they are building a kingdom? None, for they were not considered equals; little children were irrelevant and more of a nuisance for twelve men tasked with building a great kingdom.

Who else might those twelve treat as unworthy of honor? Peter revealed the answer to that question when he asked about the person who kept sinning against him. How long would Jesus expect him to put up with such a person? Surely, there would come a time when Peter could write that relationship off. How about after the seventh sin? To invest time in a person was a way to give them honor, and seven times was a lot of honor. Surely, a person who kept wronging someone else did not deserve such honor.

Is this then the thread that runs through the teaching? Take a moment and read the encounters Jesus had after this block of teachings. Was a man expected to honor his wife and marriage covenant if he was displeased with her (19:1-12)? Did the disciples have to honor children by giving them time with Jesus for a blessing (19:13-15)? Should a rich man care enough about the poor to sell his possessions and honor them with a share of his wealth (19:16-30)? Jesus told a parable that showed that those who came later into the kingdom were just as worthy of the same honor as those who came in earlier (20:1-16). Jesus instructed his disciples again that he was willing to give up everything for his mission and would die for it, thus bestowing honor on those he died for (20:17-19). Jesus corrected James and John when their mother directly sought honor and greatness for her sons (20:20-28). Jesus stopped his march to Jerusalem and spent time healing and honoring two blind men who were irrelevant to everybody else (20:29-34).

I believe the question of who is worthy of honor runs throughout the teachings and the encounters afterward. That honor was given to others by putting them before self. Jesus did not want his followers to be like culture and value self over others. His followers were called to go counter-culture on this.

I should take some time to prevent my words from being misunderstood and misapplied at this point. There is a dynamic that has become more exposed in our times, known as domestic violence. Should we take Jesus' teachings in this section to impose on a victim of domestic violence a command to stay in that relationship as a way to honor their marriage covenant? No. The abuser has already dishonored the marriage covenant and the spouse through the abuse. The guilt of dishonoring a spouse and treating her/him as disposable rests on the abuser, not the abused. Fleeing abuse, especially to protect children, does not violate Jesus' teachings.

The Pursuit of Honor (18:1)

When Jesus gave his first teachings on the mountain, his twelve chosen followers heard his indictment of the Pharisees and the teachers of the law regarding how they pursued honor. Jesus' teachings could not have been clearer. Yet the twelve followers did not apply these teachings to themselves. In their minds, they were engaging in the culturally accepted way to gain honor. The Pharisees and teachers of the law were rebuked by Jesus because they pursued honor hypocritically. These twelve followers of Jesus did not see themselves as being hypocritical. The pursuit of honor was important in their culture. Every man not only desired to be honored, but was expected to pursue it.

In that ancient Jewish culture, there was only so much honor to spread around, so the only way a man in that culture could gain more honor was if some other man lost honor to him in a public setting. When the twelve followers asked Jesus who was the greatest in his kingdom of heaven, they were not trying to gain honor for themselves by taking it from Jesus. They knew he was the leader. What they were attempting to do was to take honor from the other eleven to gain more for themselves. This was the thinking of good Jewish men of that time: gaining honor at others' expense.

If those twelve men could get Jesus, their leader, to acknowledge which of them would be his right-hand man in the kingdom, in the presence of the other eleven, then this transfer of honor would happen. The twelve expected Jesus would name one of them. It is important to note that these twelve men were not trying to trap Jesus or bait him.

According to their culture, they were engaging in a noble and open pursuit of honor.

One problem with this pursuit of honor by cultural means was that each contestant would see the other person as less significant. It did not matter what shame or embarrassment attached itself to the loser in the honor challenge. If they lost honor, they deserved to be less significant. This attitude was an area where Jesus went counter-culture; it did not fit into his kingdom.

Before we move further into Jesus' teachings, we need to reflect on where these teachings hit our hearts. How do we pursue honor? To whom do we give honor, and from whom do we withhold it? Let's ask these questions not as citizens of our culture, but as followers of Jesus. Do we follow Jesus' teachings, or do we mimic our culture?

Let's consider the quest for honor. Honor is not a bad thing, to be sure; it was not for Jesus, and it is not in his kingdom. The concern arises over how we seek to acquire it. Do our efforts lift up ourselves and tear others down? Do we treat others as unimportant as we pursue our honor? Or do we see ourselves as less important and lift others up as we pursue honor?

I recall an event after terrorists attacked the United States on September 11, 2001. On that day, thousands were killed, more were injured, and countless numbers were grieving. It was a strange time for this country in the days and weeks that followed. Slowly, people began to find a way forward.

All over the country, communities started to find their way forward by remembering and honoring the fallen, the heroes, and the broken through civic assemblies. I attended one of those gatherings in a small community. In this one, the mayor asked a teenage girl to sing the national anthem to start things off. Then he had several local leaders speak. He had a local preacher and a local priest offer up prayers. After that, he invited any other preachers and priests present to come up and offer prayers as well.

I sat and watched these preachers line up and come to the microphone. I witnessed something good morph into something unseemly. Each preacher came to the microphone to pray, but before praying, each gave some rendition about where he was and what he was doing when he heard about the attacks. The assembly heard one personal story after another that lifted up each preacher. The prayers each preacher offered were grandiose and flowery, as if each was trying to out-pray the others in the public eye. I don't know if this is what any of them intended, but it is what evolved. The focus had moved away from those intended to be honored to the preachers. It seemed like a public contest for these preachers to gain honor.

There was one preacher who refrained, though. He felt uncomfortable joining that procession and was content to pass the invitation by. When all the preachers had finished their speeches and prayers, the mayor approached the microphone and noticed that remaining preacher sitting there silently. The mayor politely invited that preacher to close out the proceedings with a prayer. That preacher did so, without making any speech, without flowery language, and keeping the focus on others for whom he was asked to pray.

That image stands out for me as two ways to gain honor. Only one was the kingdom way, the one that humbled self and lifted others up. Perhaps you have your own recollections of witnessing the pursuit of honor in ways that lifted up self and not others. Maybe others were even hurt, yet it did not matter to the one who had gained honor at their expense. Maybe it was the quest for recognition and promotion at work. Maybe it was the quest for some elected office. Maybe it was the simple desire to build oneself up in the eyes of others by knocking somebody down on the social ladder.

We have grown accustomed to these things happening in culture. Perhaps we are even accustomed to it happening in churches. We need to remember Jesus' teachings, though, because he will never get accustomed to it. Some people seeking public honor in the wrong ways may find out they will miss out on the kingdom. That could even be true of disciples.

Jesus' Rebuke and Initial Response (18:2-14)

How strongly did Jesus feel about what he would teach his twelve followers, the ones he had personally chosen? You are about to hear the depth of his convictions. Jesus summoned a small child and had that child stand in the midst of those twelve men and himself. Then he looked those twelve men in the eyes and said to each one of them: *Truly I tell you, unless you change and become like little children, you will never enter the kingdom of heaven.* In earlier teachings, Jesus said the Pharisees and the teachers of the law would not make it into his kingdom as they were. Now he was telling his twelve followers, his new teachers of the law, that they were on a road that would cause them to miss the kingdom as well.

That had to be a cold slap in the face to those twelve men. They had totally misread Jesus; in fact, they had not really even heard him. Each of them thought they were on track to be Jesus' right-hand man, and it turns out, they were on the verge of being excluded from the kingdom. Their thinking would put them on the wrong road. In order to avoid this terrible fate, they had to undergo a radical change in their thinking. They had to go counter-culture as well. What they had been raised to believe was honorable was despised in the kingdom they wanted to enter.

Jesus used the little child to teach his twelve more about honor than they had bargained for. First, he had them look at the child, knowing they had probably overlooked the child from the start. Instead of placing them as models for the child, he placed the child as a model for them. How so? In that Jewish culture, little children were not caught up in the pursuit of honor. At such a young age, they were focused on other things, like eating, sleeping, or playing. Honor was not the concern of little children. Jesus wanted his twelve to embrace the attitude of a small child in that culture, an attitude that was not consumed with acquiring honor at the expense of others. They had to jettison that way of pursuing honor or miss the kingdom altogether. There was no need to worry about being the right-hand man in a kingdom if they were not even part of it.

Jesus did not stop there, though. He went on to teach his twelve even more lessons about children that they needed to learn. Not only should they use them as a role model in this matter of pursuing honor, but they should also welcome them. Children were important people in the kingdom; they were not little nuisances to ignore and push off on someone else. It would not take long to find out that the twelve followers missed this lesson (Matthew 19:13-15). Attitudes that were ingrained in these twelve men from their youth were not easily tossed aside and could pop back up very quickly. These attitudes were truly hard to get rid of, but so necessary to be free from.

Even more importantly, these followers needed to make sure they did not cause any child to stumble. Did those twelve men actually cause children to stumble? Probably not deliberately or even knowingly. However, if they did not see children as people deserving notice and honor, they could easily hurt a child and cause him or her to stumble. This lesson was so critical that Jesus elaborated more on it. For instance, if anyone caused a child to stumble, they would be better off being drowned in the sea. If they had some attitude about children that would cause them to stumble, they needed to cut it out of their lives or face being sent to hell for actually causing a child to stumble. Going further, Jesus informed them that children were so honored by the Father in heaven that he gave each of them an angel to watch over them. Since those angels were always before the Father, the twelve could be sure the Father would know who, when, and how that child was caused to stumble. The implication was that no one would escape judgment for such a heinous evil.

To make sure the twelve understood how much the Father in heaven valued and honored children, Jesus told them a parable about a shepherd going after a lost sheep. In the parable, the lost sheep was a child that had wandered off (stumbled). The shepherd left ninety-nine other sheep to fend for themselves so that he could find that lost lamb. He did not stop looking until he found it, and he celebrated more over that lone sheep than over the ninety-nine that never wandered off. In case the twelve did not understand the parable, Jesus explained it to them: *the Father in heaven does not want to lose one child he has created.* Likely those twelve men, at least momentarily, were uncomfortably aware of how they had not honored children. Perhaps they even looked differently at that little child standing in front of them.

Now we turn our focus to how we treat children. How do children fit into our worldview as adult disciples? When we are involved in kingdom work, where do the children fit in? Perhaps your experience is different from mine, but mine has been mixed. I have seen adult disciples go all in for Vacation Bible Schools, summer camps, and helping youth homes. I have known disciples who gave up vacation time, donated gracious amounts of money and resources, and who would drop everything else if they knew a child who needed their help. I have also experienced sitting through weekly church announcements where there was an ongoing plea for some adults, any adults, to help staff a nursery or to help with some form of a children's worship. I have seen churches struggle with getting Bible school teachers because adults were afraid they would get stuck with the children and not be able to go to an adult class again.

To honor children often requires giving up self so that their needs can be met. When some followers understand this, we see beautiful things happen, and children are greatly blessed. When only a few understand this, then we see reluctance and burnout and children being treated like a burden. This is why we need to make sure every follower of Jesus hears his teachings about children.

I know a woman disciple of Jesus who longed to be in the main worship time of her church. She longed to be fed spiritually at her adult level. Yet, she was tired of hearing the endless announcements, week after week, of a need for someone to lead the children's worship during that time. She decided that if no one else would answer the call, she would. That began a years-long experience of her carrying out that ministry for the children. Why years long? Sadly, some of it was because nobody else was willing to serve in that capacity. Incredibly, it also was because this woman came to a point where she did not want to give it up. She loved those children, and God was nurturing her in other ways through them. She lived out Jesus' teaching of welcoming and looking after children and was greatly blessed.

Reflecting on another part of Jesus' teachings, it is surely a counter-cultural view to see little children as role models when it comes to the pursuit of honor. We all know children can be selfish and cruel to other children. Jesus knew that as well, even though he taught his disciples to become like little children. So why would he teach such a lesson? Perhaps it is because of the sweeter side of children that Jesus made them a role model for adults. We also have seen the wonder and beauty that is revealed when we watch children act unselfishly, not caring about what is in it for them but thinking of others. At those times, they touch our hearts, and we understand why Jesus would teach this.

This is a lot of counter-culture to take in, but we need to stick with Jesus a while longer and apply all of his teachings to us. When we look into Jesus' teachings about causing children to stumble, and children having angels that continually stand before the Father in heaven, we should feel a strong sense of being held accountable. We should have a sense of every child being a gift from God that is entrusted to us. The last thing our heavenly Father wants to see is a child wander off from him. The last thing God wants to do is bring judgment on those children because they wandered off from him. So he will do everything he can to find them and save them before that happens, and he will hold accountable all who are responsible for these little ones wandering away from him.

Is it not remarkable that every child has a pure love and heartfelt joy when they get to be part of Bible classes, Vacation Bible Schools, Children's Church, and the like? This is not just because those things are fun; the reason runs deeper. Children are still in tune with the Creator. In their innocence, they have a connection with him. They love God. They love hearing his stories and singing songs about him. They love Jesus. They have a passion in them for God that we did not put there; we only nurture it. How terrible it is then, when we do something that kills that passion for God.

What will the Father in heaven do with those adults who cause the children who believe in him to stumble and to wander off? We are informed that he will bring his judgment upon those adults responsible. Those were the *drowning with a millstone* and *fire of hell* parts of Jesus' teaching. Is that a sobering thought that gets our attention? It should. We should give thought to the countless ways we have seen children harmed that led them to wandering off from the Father. How can we think it goes unnoticed by the Father when we degrade his children by emotionally, physically, sexually, or verbally abusing them? This is spiritual abuse to which the Father will not turn a blind eye. When a child who believes in Jesus stops believing because of some way an adult treated him or her, Jesus had no compassionate or comforting words for that person. Could that person repent and change their heart and ways? Surely so, but that person should know it would be of utmost importance to do so quickly. Millstones and fires of hell might come upon them quickly if they do not. The Father watches his children and knows everything that is done to them; we need to remember this.

Perhaps there are adult disciples who draw back from any ministry to children because this is so serious. No doubt, there are people who should not be involved in children's ministry because they have some character trait that is spiritually flawed. Those people are wise to avoid such ministry and allow God to heal them and use them in other kingdom works. However, children cannot be totally avoided in the kingdom, for they are part of it. So every follower of Jesus needs to be sure his or her attitudes and actions towards those children are what their Lord expects them to be.

A Further Response about Honoring Others (18:15-20)

If Jesus was giving teachings to people who wanted to follow him, teachings about how to follow and what was involved, can we expect warm and fuzzy teachings that soothe us and promise us rainbows and ice cream? So far, we have not found that to be the case; in fact, we have heard the opposite. Why is that?

It is not because Jesus is some sort of masochist who likes to see his followers go through extreme pain and suffering. That does not align at all with his teachings on love and his life example of loving, especially the unloved. The reason for such hard teachings is that the enemy of Jesus—Satan—has so twisted and perverted this world that any movement that furthers holiness and love is going to be widely rejected and opposed. Jesus' kingdom spreads by taking "ground" from the enemy, and that enemy does not surrender anything or anyone without a fight. The enemy has so ingrained his values in the cultures of this world that any teaching of Jesus is going to be counter-cultural. This means his teachings will always be hard, and traveling the road Jesus walked will always be difficult and dangerous. We follow Jesus down this road not because it is easy, but because it is the only road that leads to life (check out John 6:60-69).

We should not be surprised, then, that Jesus challenges his culture, and ours, with an even more radical teaching about honoring others. We may have problems with consistently honoring children, welcoming them, and imitating their best qualities, but we are willing to try. Children have a lovable quality about them. However, there are some people we deem unlovable—for example, someone who wrongs us over and over again. You probably can picture in your mind the face of such a person right now. That is where Jesus' teachings take us now and where they took his first disciples then.

In Jesus' teaching, honor is given to such a person when the offended party puts forth effort to redeem the relationship. The offender may be considered unworthy by most people, but the disciple of Jesus treats them as if they are worthy by trying to bring the relationship back to a healthy place (remember, Jesus was not teaching about how to deal with an abuser). Jesus' disciples would not only attempt to bring about healing and restoration of a broken relationship, but they were instructed to do so many times in many ways. They would support one another in such efforts. This was an incredibly radical teaching in that day and culture. To be sure, it would be so in any day and any culture, but that was a time and culture when people lived by the *eye-for-an-eye and tooth-for-a-tooth* mentality. We could easily, and fairly, assume that those twelve men were listening with wide eyes and dropped jaws as they struggled to accept this teaching.

An added pill for those twelve to swallow was that the person who had been wronged would be the one to initiate this restoration, not the person guilty of doing the wrong. This teaching was not far removed from the teachings of turning the other cheek and going the extra mile. Jesus was not discharging the offender of any responsibility, but he was teaching the offended the proper response, which is all they had control over. What may have seemed backward to those twelve men actually gave them more influence on the ultimate outcome of reconciliation.

What made the pill even harder to swallow was that Jesus expected his followers to keep trying to restore the relationship even after the other person had rejected the attempts and even denied any guilt or responsibility. At that point, those twelve men may have been choking on that pill, but Jesus said his followers would honor the relationship and the guilty person more than their own pride and ego. No doubt Jesus knew how readily people would walk away from a relationship after only minimal effort to restore it. No doubt he knew how stubborn people could be in admitting their guilt. If his followers were not willing to go to such lengths to reconcile, Jesus would eventually rule a kingdom where nobody was getting along with anybody. Their surrounding culture was evidence of how people suffered because of broken relationships; his kingdom would offer a different and far superior experience simply because of his emphasis on reconciliation.

Jesus saw there would come a point when no effort of any kind would be successful in restoring a broken relationship. He did not keep his disciples on the hook indefinitely. He knew they would sometimes have to move on with a damaged relationship in their wake, but that would not result from a lack of effort on the part of his followers. There would, however, be a positive that would come out of this failed effort. The offended brothers or sisters would not walk away from the relationship filled with anger. Instead, they would feel sorrow and pain. Why would that be good? Because they were feeling love for the offender and not hate. All the effort put forth by the offended made that change inevitable. They, at least, would be in a better place when love was filling their hearts.

As Jesus wrapped up his instructions about multiple and varied efforts to honor people who had broken relationships, he informed them that they would not engage in those efforts of reconciliation alone. Indeed, Jesus and his Father would be intimately involved. That is the message in 18:18-20. These texts have confused followers and been misapplied as well. To avoid making the same mistake, we need to remember these teachings take place in the context of reconciling broken relationships.

Jesus taught those twelve men that whatever they bound on earth would be bound in heaven, and whatever they loosed on earth would be loosed in heaven. What did that teaching mean? It is fairly simple to understand when the context is considered. Whenever a disciple worked to restore a broken relationship, the Father would honor what the disciple's efforts brought about. If forgiveness and restoration occurred, the Father would honor that outcome. If a sin was forgiven and let go in order for that to occur, the Father would agree with that. If reconciliation could not come about because the guilty party refused to acknowledge his or her wrong and responsibility, the disciple had the power to proclaim that the other person's guilt still remained on them, and the disciple was no longer bound to the relationship. The Father in heaven would agree with that. This binding and loosing on earth would be recognized and honored by the Father in heaven.

Jesus further promised that whenever these disciples came together to work on the restoration of the relationship, he would be right there, in the thick of it, with them. This part of his teaching wasn't about Jesus being with two or three disciples whenever they came together to worship, though there is no reason to doubt that. Rather, it was the setting of those disciples coming together to work on reconciliation. This is so important to Jesus that he promised to be intimately involved in that effort.

These last teachings had some pretty big ramifications. For starters, any restoration that would occur would be a sacred experience because of the involvement of the Father and Son with the disciples. Reconciliation would not be just a human effort, and the impact would not be limited to just the earthly realm. Furthermore, both the Father and the Son were giving significant power to the followers of Jesus to bring forgiveness or judgment on other people. That was given to Jesus' followers in another set of teachings and in another setting (Matthew 10:12-15). Jesus gave honor and respect to his followers when he empowered them to make such judgments that could bring either a blessing or a curse. For Jesus, restoring broken relationships with people who did not deserve that honor was a pretty big deal; he wanted his disciples to have the same value, so he gave them the tools they would need if they just had the same heart as he did.

Do we share this value with our Teacher? Will we extend honor to the person who has wronged us and has not asked for forgiveness? They do not deserve the honor, but that is not the criterion Jesus sets before us. We give them this honor because Jesus instructed us to. Just as he embodied his teaching on the cross, he expects his disciples to embody it in their lives even when it hurts. This teaching challenges us greatly because we want to write these kinds of people off like many in our culture do.

Maybe we will give lip service to the teaching by making a minimal and insincere effort towards reconciling. Do you remember when one of your parents had you apologize and make up with a brother or sister you were angry with, or maybe with a friend? You went through the motions of making up because you had to; maybe you even hugged or shook hands. However, you didn't really mean any of it. That sums us up, doesn't it? However, when we have to keep trying, and even bring others into the process, we have to get real and get real honest in our efforts. We move well beyond lip service into sincere efforts and desires for reconciliation. Hopefully, the efforts we go through will change the heart of our offender. The efforts will definitely change ours.

We have seen examples of this in the news at times. We were shocked, confused, maybe even angry, when we witnessed followers of Jesus do what culture could not imagine or even tolerate. When Brandt Jean publicly forgave Amber Guyger in a courtroom for killing his brother, Botham, in October 2019 (this included hugging her as she sobbed in his embrace), culture was shocked. Some were even angry.

In October 2006, after Charles Roberts went into a Pennsylvania one-room schoolhouse and shot ten Amish girls, killing five of them, he shot and killed himself. The cultures of this world were shocked when they witnessed how the Amish community honored the family of Charles Roberts. They showed up at Charles Roberts' funeral to show support for his parents. They reached out with love and looked beyond their pain to offer healing and reconciliation between families. They gave honor to parents whom many had already judged and deemed as unworthy of such.

Not in the news are the countless acts of disciples of Jesus giving honor to people who have wronged them; they do so by working hard to forgive and restore the broken relationships. What seems totally impossible in our culture has been shown to be very possible when one truly follows Jesus down this hard road. Those who follow these teachings do not escape pain, but they do experience the remarkable and beautiful because Jesus meets them there and gets involved.

Not every effort towards reconciliation is successful, for the guilty person has some say in the result. Forgiveness can be given by the offended, but the relationship may not be restored due to the offender refusing to acknowledge guilt and responsibility, or because they refuse to change. Sometimes the best efforts cannot avoid that outcome today, any more than it could for those first twelve followers. That does not mean the effort was in vain, though, because the disciples of Jesus will be able to move forward and experience healing and freedom from anger and hatred. That is the power that Jesus brings into these efforts.

When the guilty refuse to reconcile by accepting responsibility or by changing, what happens to them? Not only do they suffer the loss of the relationship, but they also face the judgment of the Father in heaven, who honors what the followers of Jesus bound and loosed. That will not be good for those who rejected the efforts of reconciliation by Jesus' followers.

We Get What We Give (18:21-35)

How did Jesus wind up his fourth block of teaching? With a parable, of course. Those stories were excellent ways to drive his teachings home, and Jesus was skilled at telling them.

What prompted the parable from Jesus was a question that one of his followers had asked him: *How many times should I forgive someone who keeps doing me wrong? Is seven enough?* That question was asked by Peter, and it was a fair question to ask. Surely seven times would be showing enough mercy. Anybody who needed more forgiveness than that surely did not deserve the honor of being forgiven again. Jesus thought they did, however. He gave an even larger amount of forgiveness to Peter for his consideration, but the number was not the point. Jesus' teaching was that his disciples should never shut the door on forgiving others. The parable explains why.

The focal point of the story is a servant who owed more debt than he could pay his master. We would say his debt was astronomical, one that would have been impossible to pay back. When faced with severe judgment by the king to recoup his losses, the servant begged for mercy and received it. Having been forgiven, the servant was released. Upon his release, he encountered a fellow servant who owed him a far less amount of money. Even when his fellow servant begged for mercy, the first servant refused to show it and cast the man in prison until he could pay his debt. The actions of this unmerciful servant led to a chain reaction in which he was brought back before his master and received an even worse judgment than what he had meted out to his fellow servant.

The point of the parable is clear: those who have been given mercy should be willing to give it. Otherwise, they will receive the judgment they give out. Jesus told his disciples they should give out what they had received, or they would get what they gave out. When you get mercy, give mercy. If you get mercy and fail to give mercy, then you will get the judgment you gave out.

The application of the parable is where those twelve would have been humbled. In the application, the unmerciful servant was Peter and the other eleven followers. Jesus cast his disciples as the bad guys of his story. The king was the Father in heaven. Already the dynamic of the parable is shocking because Jesus is casting his follower as the one who did wrong so many times that he had amassed an unpayable debt to God. The fellow servant was significant, too. He represented the unworthy person that Peter had asked about, the one who had wronged him seven times. In the parable, he is the one the hearer has pity on, and the first servant is the one the hearers get angry with. We can be pretty sure that Peter and his fellow disciples did not like this parable.

What the parable brought to the forefront was that these twelve men, even though they had been chosen by Jesus to be his teachers, were no angels. They were the kind of men who had needed forgiveness many times over. They were twelve men who had sinned over and over again and who were worthy of judgment from the Father in heaven. However, the Father had forgiven them of all they had done wrong. How could they then turn around and refuse to give mercy to someone who had done less to them than they had done to the Father in heaven? This reality reframed the whole question about who needed forgiveness and how often it should be granted.

As hard as it must have been for those twelve men to hear that parable, what Jesus said next was even harder. We recall the very harsh rebuke Jesus had for his followers when he started his teaching: *"Unless you change and become like little children, you will never enter the kingdom."* That statement packed a terrifying punch. Jesus closed out his teachings with a statement that was no less terrifying: *"This is how my heavenly Father will treat each of you unless you forgive your brother or sister from your heart."* That statement came on the heels of the story where the king was so angry, he turned the unmerciful servant over to the jailers to be tortured. Jesus was not just asking his followers to be forgiving people; he was demanding it. More than that, their forgiveness toward people who needed it over and over again had to be sincere. If they would not go that far with their forgiveness, then those disciples would face terrible judgment from the Father in heaven.

In this fourth block of teaching, Jesus gave absolutely no room for his disciples to catch their breath. He saw the culture those men lived in, and he knew their hearts. He knew they had to undergo some radical change if they were going to live out, as well as teach, his message about the kingdom. He knew he was sending those followers out on a mission where they could easily become hardened and unforgiving. If that happened, they would lose a defining character trait Jesus wanted in all of his followers. That could not happen, and Jesus would not allow it.

As I look over this parable, I find it easier to digest than Jesus' final statement. The parable is hard to live out, to be sure, but not impossible. Jesus never called his followers to attempt the impossible; all of his teachings are within the reach of people's abilities to follow. I have noticed, though, that Jesus' last statement does not get a lot of attention. It is almost like Jesus never said it. Preachers and teachers will walk people through the parable and hardly, if ever, focus on the last statement.

In practice, I have seen Christians make a pretense of forgiving others with empty words, but it was easy to see their hearts were not in those words; it was even easier to see when there were no actions that backed up their words. They never considered that the failure to be sincere in forgiving others put their own souls in danger. They never seemed to consider that the Father in heaven could see through their empty words. Nor did those Christians seem to factor in how much their Father had forgiven them, and that alone was the reason they should give the same mercy to others.

When you reflect on this block of Jesus' teachings, it would be time well spent to reflect on any relationships that have been broken in your life, and perhaps some of them remain broken. Take out your pen and paper and write down the names of those people. As you look at the names, see their faces. Recall what happened to break the relationship, if you can even remember. Then think about this: what emotion would you feel if you unexpectedly came face-to-face with that person today? If that emotion makes you uncomfortable and uneasy, perhaps the Spirit is revealing something to you. Perhaps you need to spend some time considering how you can forgive that person in your heart. If you find a way to do that, my belief is you will experience some special and freeing blessing. Jesus knows what he is talking about; disciples just need to learn how to trust him and put his teachings into practice.

As we wrap up this fourth block of teaching from Jesus, we should come away with a clearer picture of what honor really is: how it is given, who it is given to, and why it is given. These are very humbling and very hard teachings from Jesus. The Bible is filled with teachings about the importance placed by God on how people treat other people. It should not surprise us that Jesus comes down so forcefully in these teachings about honor. If we actually hear Jesus, we will do better walking down this road of discipleship.

Seat Belt Check

Perspective can make all the difference when you face a challenge. It can be the difference between success and failure. The challenge itself does not change, but a different perspective enables you to see the challenge and approach it differently.

I will paint a picture for you, and then I will ask you a question: *Would you want to be there?* This is just a simple exercise in perspective. Here's the picture:

You see a cabin in a clearing in some northern woods. The cabin, the ground, and the trees are blanketed in heavy snow. There are no visible roads, but you see part of a headlight of a car that is barely visible; otherwise, the car is buried in snow. There are long icicles hanging from every section of the cabin roof. You see an old-fashioned thermometer on the front porch of the cabin, but you see no red in the thermometer, and there are icicles hanging from it. You know it is bitter cold.

You see trees swaying and snow swirling, so you know a strong, cold wind is blowing. It is night, but the skies are clear and filled with stars. In the dark edges of the picture, you can make out the images of a pack of hungry wolves lurking about. They are pacing back and forth, looking for any opportunity to eat anything they can.

Looking closer at the cabin, you see wisps of smoke coming from the chimney. You see a yellow glow coming out of the windows. Looking through the dingy windows, you see a roaring fireplace.

Gathered around the fireplace are adults and children, smiling and drinking from mugs that have traces of steam rising from them.

This is the picture. *Would you want to be there?* That depends on what the dominant image is that you are focused on in the picture. Is it the deep snow, the icicles, the chilling wind, the thermometer, the car buried in snow, the lack of a visible road out, the hungry pack of wolves? Or is it the warm glow in the windows, the roaring fire, the smiling faces, the happy children, the hot mugs of some drink? What you focus on is your perspective of the picture. Your perspective determines how you answer the question.

The same is true about following Jesus. If you focus on the hard aspects such as the challenges, going counter-culture, the opposition, and the mistreatment that will come your way, you will not want to be there. If, however, you focus on the blessings of restored relationships, deeper and quality connections, and the back-and-forth flow of honor, you will want to be there. The right perspective is a good seat belt to wear.

Matthew 24-25
Fifth Block of Teaching

24 Jesus left the temple and was walking away when his disciples came up to him to call his attention to its buildings. ² "Do you see all these things?" he asked. "Truly I tell you, not one stone here will be left on another; every one will be thrown down."

³As Jesus was sitting on the Mount of Olives, the disciples came to him privately. "Tell us," they said, "when will this happen, and what will be the sign of your coming and of the end of the age?"

⁴Jesus answered, "Watch out that no one deceives you. ⁵For many will come in my name, claiming, 'I am the Messiah,' and will deceive many. ⁶You will hear of wars and rumors of wars, but see to it that you are not alarmed. Such things must happen, but the end is still to come. ⁷Nation will rise against nation, and kingdom against kingdom. There will be famines and earthquakes in various places. ⁸All these are the beginning of birth pains.

⁹"Then you will be handed over to be persecuted and put to death, and you will be hated by all nations because of me. ¹⁰At that time many will turn away from the faith and will betray and hate each other, ¹¹and many false prophets will appear and deceive many people. ¹²Because of the increase of wickedness, the love of most will grow cold, ¹³but the one who stands firm to the end will be saved. ¹⁴And this gospel of the kingdom will be preached to the whole world as a testimony to all nations, and then the end will come.

¹⁵"So when you see standing in the holy place 'the abomination that causes desolation,' spoken of through the prophet Daniel - let the reader understand - ¹⁶then let those who are in Judea flee to the mountains. ¹⁷Let no one on the housetop go down to take anything out of the house. ¹⁸Let no one in the field go back to get their cloak. ¹⁹How dreadful it will be in those days for pregnant women and nursing mothers! ²⁰Pray that your flight will not take place in winter or on the Sabbath. ²¹For then there will be great distress, unequaled from the beginning of the world until now - and never to be equaled again.

²²"If those days had not been cut short, no one would survive, but for the the sake of the elect, those days will be shortened. ²³At that time if anyone says to you, 'Look, here is the Messiah!' or 'There he is!' do not believe it. ²⁴For false messiahs and false prophets will appear and perform great signs and wonders to deceive, if possible, even the elect. ²⁵See, I have told you ahead of time.

²⁶"So if anyone tells you, 'There he is, out in the wilderness,' do not go out; or 'Here he is, in the inner rooms,' do not believe it. ²⁷For as lightning that comes from the east is visible in the west, so will it be with the coming of the Son of Man. ²⁸Wherever there is a carcass, there the vultures will gather.

²⁹"Immediately after the distress of those days

" ' the sun will be darkened,

and the moon will not give its light;

The stars will fall from the sky,

and the heavenly bodies will be shaken,'

30"Then will appear the sign of the Son of Man in heaven. And then all the peoples of the earth will mourn for they will see the Son of Man coming on the clouds of heaven, with power and great glory. 31And he will send his angels with a loud trumpet call, and they will gather his elect from the four winds, from one end of the heavens to the other.

32"Now learn this lesson from the fig tree: As soon as its twigs get tender and the leaves come out, you know that summer is near. 33Even so, when you see all of these things, you know it is near, right at the door. 34Truly, I tell you, this generation will certainly not pass away until all these things have happened. 35Heaven and earth will pass away, but my words will never pass away.

36"But about that day or hour no one knows, not even the angels in heaven, nor the Son, but only the Father. 37As it was in the days of Noah, so it will be at the coming of the Son of Man. 38For in the days before the flood, people were eating and drinking, marrying and giving in marriage, up to the day Noah entered the ark, 39and they knew nothing about what would happen until the flood came and took them all away. That is how it will be with the coming of the Son of Man. 40Two men will be working in the field; one will be taken and the other left. 41Two women will be grinding with a hand mill; one will be taken and the other left.

42"Therefore, keep watch, because you do not know on what day your Lord will come. 43But understand this: If the owner of the house had known at what time the thief was coming, he would have kept watch all night and would not have let his house be broken into. ⁴⁴So you also must be ready, because the Son of Man will come at an hour when you do not expect him.

⁴⁵"Who then is the faithful and wise servant, whom the master has left in charge of the servants in his household to give them their food at the proper time? ⁴⁶It will be good for the servant whose master finds him doing so when he returns. ⁴⁷Truly I tell you, he will put him charge of all of his possessions. ⁴⁸But suppose that servant is wicked and says to himself, 'My master is staying away a long time,' ⁴⁹and he then begins to beat his fellow servants and to eat and drink with drunkards. ⁵⁰The master of that servant will come on a day when he does not expect him and at an hour he is not aware of. ⁵¹He will cut him to pieces and assign him a place with the hypocrites, where there will be weeping and gnashing of teeth.

25 "At that time the kingdom of heaven will be like ten virgins who took their lamps and went out to meet the bridegroom. ²Five of them were foolish and five were wise. ³The foolish ones took their lamps but did not take any oil with them. ⁴The wise ones, however, took oil in jars along with their lamps. ⁵The bridegroom was a long time in coming, and they all became drowsy and fell asleep.

⁶"At midnight the cry rang out: 'Here's the bridegroom! Come out to meet him!'

⁷"Then all the virgins awoke and trimmed their lamps. ⁸The foolish ones said to the wise, 'Give us some of your oil; our lamps are going out.'

⁹" 'No,' they replied, 'there may not be enough for both us and you. Instead, go to those who sell oil and buy some for yourselves.'

¹⁰"But while they were on their way to buy the oil, the bridegroom arrived. The virgins who were ready went in with him to the wedding banquet. And the door was shut.

¹¹"Later the others also came. 'Lord, Lord,' they said, 'open the door for us!'

¹²"But he replied, 'Truly I tell you, I don't know you.'

¹³"Therefore keep watch, because you do not know the day or the hour.

¹⁴"Again, it will be like a man going on a journey, who called his servants and entrusted his wealth to them. ¹⁵To one he gave five bags of gold, to another two bags, and to another one bag, each according to his ability. Then he went on his journey. ¹⁶The man who had received the five bags of gold went at once and gained five bags more. ¹⁷So also the man who had been given two bags of gold gained two more. ¹⁸But the man who had received one bag went off, dug a hole in the ground and hid his master's money.

¹⁹"After a long time the master of those servants returned and settled accounts with them. ²⁰The man who had received the five bags of gold brought the other five. 'Master,' he said, 'you entrusted me with five bags of gold. See I have gained five more.'

²¹"His master replied, 'Well done, good and faithful servant! You have been faithful with a few things; I will put you in charge of many things. Come and share your master's happiness!'

²²"The man with the two bags of gold also came. 'Master,' he said, 'you entrusted me with two bags of gold; see I have gained two more.'

²³"His master replied, 'Well done, good and faithful servant!' You have been faithful with a few things; I will put you in charge of many things. Come and share your master's happiness!'

²⁴"Then the man who had received one bag of gold came. 'Master,' he said, 'I knew that you are a hard man, harvesting where you have not sown and gathering where you have not scattered seed. ²⁵So I was afraid and went out and hid your gold. See, here is what belongs to you.'

²⁶"His master replied, 'You wicked, lazy servant! So you knew that I harvest where I have not sown and gather where I have not scattered seed? ²⁷Well then, you should have put my money on deposit with the bankers, so that when I returned I would have received it back with interest.

²⁸" 'So take the bag of gold from him and give it to the one who has ten bags. ²⁹For whoever has will be given more, and they will have an abundance. Whoever does not have, even what they have will be taken from them. ³⁰And throw that worthless servant outside, into the darkness, where there will be weeping and gnashing of teeth.

³¹"When the Son of Man comes in glory, and all the angels with him, he will sit on his glorious throne. ³²All the nations will be gathered before

him, and he will separate the people one from another, as a shepherd separates the sheep from the goats. ³³He will put the sheep on his right and the goats on his left.

³⁴"Then the King will say to those on his right, 'Come, you who are blessed by my Father; take your inheritance, the kingdom prepared for you since the creation of the world. ³⁵For I was hungry and you gave me something to eat, I was thirsty and you gave me something to drink, I was a stranger and you invited me in, ³⁶I needed clothes and you clothed me, I was sick and you looked after me, I was in prison and you came to visit me.

³⁷"Then the righteous will answer him, 'Lord, when did we see you hungry and feed you, or thirsty and give you something to drink? ³⁸When did we see you a stranger and invite you in, or needing clothes and clothe you? ³⁹When did we see you sick or in prison and go to visit you?

⁴⁰"The King will reply, 'Truly I tell you, whatever you did for one of the least of these brothers and sisters of mine, you did for me.'

⁴¹"Then he will say to those on his left, 'Depart from me, you who are cursed, into the eternal fire prepared for the devil and his angels. ⁴²For I was hungry and you gave me nothing to eat, I was thirsty and you gave me nothing to drink, ⁴³I was a stranger and you did not invite me in, I was sick and in prison and you did not look after me.'

44"They also will answer, 'Lord, when did we see you hungry or thirsty or a stranger or needing clothes or sick or in prison, and did not help you?'

45"He will reply, 'Truly I tell you, whatever you did not do for one of the least of these, you did not do for me.'

46"Then they will go away to eternal punishment, but the righteous to eternal life.

Prepping for the Teaching

We come now to the fifth and final block of teachings in Matthew's gospel, where Jesus focused on teaching his disciples how to follow him. What will we find? We should expect to find more difficult teachings, for none have been easy so far. We should expect to hear Jesus teach lessons that we need to hear. Perhaps they will be lessons we have not been told before, which may have been the case for you in some of the other blocks of teaching. We are going straight to the authoritative source to learn how to walk this road and look directly to Jesus as we read his very words. Let's not be put off by hard teachings we need to hear.

Let's approach this final block of teaching from Jesus as we have the earlier ones. Take whatever time you need to read them, and read through them as many times as you need. Again, we are in no rush. Become familiar with what Jesus said. Jot down some notes about what impressed you about his teachings. You could even write down any questions that come to your mind as you read. Those questions can be helpful guides for you. When you are ready, you can pick up here again, and we will move forward.

The Thread that Runs Through

Take a look with me at what happened to prompt this block of teaching. From what we read, we see that the twelve are with Jesus at the temple in Jerusalem. Like every Jew of that time, the temple was a great source of national pride, and many regarded it as one of the wonders of the world. If a Jew went to Jerusalem, the temple was a site they had to visit. This was where the Lord God lived.

There was more to the appeal of the temple than God's presence, though. Herod the Great had done a major renovation of the temple mount. All of it was a grand structure that awed the people. Many of the stones were massive in size and weight, dwarfing the people standing next to them. The smallest stones weighed somewhere between two to five tons; the largest were probably over five hundred tons. Herod the Great made sure the temple would be an awesome spectacle for all who saw it. Most of the Jewish people would have rejoiced when Herod died because they did not like him. However, every one of them would have regarded Herod's work on the temple mount as one thing he did right.

We should not be surprised, then, when Jesus' twelve followers came up to him to engage in a conversation about how glorious the temple was. Surely this would have been the time to have a pleasant conversation with Jesus. After all, by now they believed him to be God's Son. If God lived in the temple, then surely Jesus would love the structure as much as they did. Surely, he too would be impressed by what he saw. However, Jesus showed no awe or amazement at what he saw; instead, he spoke of it all being torn down.

Jesus' disturbing response prompted the disciples to seek him out later, in private. They asked for more insight and understanding. They wanted to know what was behind Jesus' lack of caring about the temple as much as they did, and that led into what they heard next. We won't get into that yet because we are focused for now on finding a thread that runs through the teaching.

Take a quick jump to the last part of Jesus' teaching in this block. You read in Matthew 25:31-46 another parable from Jesus. It is actually the last of a series of three that are connected. We will look at that connection in due time, but for now, let's notice the focus of the last parable. The parable taught what would ultimately make an impression on Jesus: how his disciples treat the least of the people they meet.

That is our thread: care about people, not buildings. What impressed Jesus was not buildings, not even the temple. In fact, prior to his teaching, he had pronounced to the crowds and his disciples that the temple would be desolated (Matthew 23:38), an event reminiscent of what happened in the days of the prophet Ezekiel. Instead, Jesus drew his followers' attention toward people that many would dismiss or oppress. Jesus wanted his disciples to focus on people, not buildings.

As we move through this last block of Jesus' teachings, we will see how Jesus moves from talking about buildings to drawing his followers' focus to the least of people. Following the thread will help us understand the teachings. So buckle in for what is likely to be a bumpy ride. I don't want to lose you now after having come so far together.

The Appeal (24:3)

The unexpected and foreboding remarks from Jesus about the temple shook the twelve. They knew their history, the time when the temple was destroyed in the days of Ezekiel and Jeremiah. Many of their people had died then. Were such dark days ahead of them again? If they were following the promised one, the Messiah, how could this be? They had heard Jesus speak often about end times and judgment. Was this all tied together? They needed to talk with Jesus further about this.

The disciples waited until their group had left the city and had gone to the Mount of Olives. There they sought out Jesus. They wanted a private audience with him when they sought their answers. In that private setting, they asked Jesus to explain to them what was coming and when.

Perhaps you understand why those followers chose to have this encounter in private. You have had your own times when you were worried about future events. You had a sense of terrible things coming your way, and you sought out someone who could give you understanding or help of some kind. You did not want a crowd around you for that conversation; you wanted to meet with just that person. If you have had such conversations, then you can feel the heaviness of the air on that night and the tenseness in the hearts of those twelve men. You know that feeling of dreading the unknown.

Tough Times for Israel (24:4-35)

One of the first distressing teachings those twelve men heard was that there would be others coming who would claim they were the Messiah. They believed Jesus was the Messiah, and for these events to happen, Jesus would have to go away. That would mean the followers would go through dark times without Jesus being physically present. How could they go through the dark times Jesus spoke of without Jesus by their side? That would make those terrible times even worse.

The twelve heard that these fakes, the false prophets, would have some form of power to persuade people. Perhaps they would be very dynamic and persuasive with their words and speeches. Perhaps they would be able to perform some miraculous acts. There would be many that would be deceived and follow them. Jesus forewarned that even his followers could be drawn in by them.

What would happen in those dark times? There would be wars on top of wars and natural disasters to live through. They would face persecution and death for Jesus. Jesus also spoke of a prophecy of Daniel that referenced a historical event when unbelievers desecrated the temple. This had happened in Daniel's day when Nebuchadnezzar's Babylonian army destroyed the temple built by Solomon. It would happen again in 70 A.D. when the Roman army would do the same thing. When that day of temple desecration came, Jesus warned all his followers to get out of Jerusalem. The terror of those days would be worse than any could imagine.

Jesus' followers would be caught up in the events, so he warned them ahead of time. It would be important for them not to put their hopes in the wrong person at that time, somebody claiming to be Jesus who had returned. They would hear those lies and wonder if they could be true, but Jesus said his return would be public enough that everybody would hear and see it.

Jesus assured those twelve that he would return. In 24:26-31, Jesus wrapped up the first half of his teaching with a promise of his return, a time when he would gather his followers and take them to be with him. So Jesus put a light at the end of that dark tunnel to encourage and strengthen his followers. This light would help protect them and keep them from being caught up by any false messiahs.

In this first part of Jesus' teachings, he focused on the events that would surround the destruction of the temple, the event he spoke of while at the temple with his followers. Toward the end, he mixed in some teachings about his return so that there would be some hope for those disciples to hang on to. At the very end of this part of his teachings (24:32-35), he answered his followers' request and told them when this would happen: during their generation's lifetime. Historically, we know that to be forty years from that night of Jesus' teachings. Jesus spoke the truth, just as he said. His words could be counted on coming to pass; they would not pass away and be forgotten.

The first half of Jesus' teaching was much more than his followers had expected. When they agreed to follow Jesus, they did not see this part of the road in their future. They would lose one key anchor of their life, the temple; they would feel like they had lost a second key anchor, Jesus. On top of that, they heard that they would suffer and die because of following Jesus. They may have even had the foresight to consider that any wives, children, family, and friends they had who were followers would suffer the same fate. How were they supposed to digest all of that? How do they even take the next step in following Jesus?

Throughout this part of the teaching, there is a question of who had the power. The empire of Rome believed they were the ultimate power because it had the armies to enforce its will. The false prophets and messiahs thought they had the power. Perhaps they had even found some power that allowed them to do wonders and miracles. They believed they would have the power to successfully lead a revolt against Rome and defeat its armies.

The followers of Jesus would find themselves suffering and dying as these powers fought one another. They might be tempted to wonder if they had trusted the right power when they followed Jesus. As Jesus spoke of his return in these teachings, he spoke of his coming back with power and glory (24:30). At that time, he would shake up the heavenly powers (bodies, 24:29). Jesus wanted his followers to know that even in the midst of terrible things happening to his followers, he had not lost power. Rome would destroy the temple and persecute and kill many of Jesus' followers. Impostors would appear to have some kind of power and lead many away from Jesus. Neither of these were real power, though, for theirs would end. The only power standing at the end would be Jesus, and he would bring all of his followers home. This is the light that Jesus offered his followers, a light that could help them to keep following him, no matter what would happen to them.

Do these teachings that referenced events which occurred almost two thousand years ago have any meaning and relevance for followers of Jesus today? I believe so. Indeed, there are a number of lessons we can take to heart.

First, Jesus was asked by his followers to explain when two things would happen: the destruction of the temple and the end of the age. What Jesus said would occur regarding the temple actually came to pass. If he was correct in those teachings, then we need to trust that his teachings about the end of the age are also true. Those words will come to pass just as certainly as his teachings about the temple's destruction did.

Second, if followers of Jesus had to go through terrible and horrific times then, we should not assume we are immune to those kinds of ordeals and suffering now. Truly, history has shown that followers of Jesus have faced persecution and death on a large scale at various times in history, all over the globe. When our terrible times come, Jesus calls us to hold firm to the end, just as he called his first disciples to do. If those followers held firm, so can we. We also need to take note and learn from those who did not stand firm so that we will not bail on Jesus. We want to tap into the best part of our heritage and walk faithfully on this road of discipleship when it gets hard for us.

Third, we can rest our hope in what Jesus offered those first followers. The hope was not in avoiding terrible times, but in getting through and beyond those terrible times. How did they do that? Rather, how will all followers do that? When Jesus returns, he will gather up all of his elect, his followers, and take them home with him. His angels will gather his disciples from all over the world, and none will be left behind. This is where Jesus' power will be unleashed. We might want his power to keep us from hurting and dying, and we know of followers who have been delivered from such. However, Jesus has not used his power in history to always deliver his followers from the terrible times. This was not because he had lost his power. He still is the dominant power, and always will be. His return is when that power will be fully revealed. This is where we need to put our hope.

I know of a man who became a follower of Jesus in a place where followers of Jesus are killed. This man's father was the chief witch doctor of the local religion. When he heard about his son becoming a follower of Jesus, he plotted to have his son killed, even using one of his daughters, the follower's own sister, to help carry out the murder. A truck was supposed to run the follower over and kill him. Instead, the driver missed the follower and killed his sister. Many other attempts have been made on this follower's life, even by some increasingly militant Muslims who are bent on killing all followers of Jesus in their country. The last I heard, this follower is alive and remains in that area proclaiming Jesus so that others can become believers. What inspires a follower to endure so much? Jesus and his ultimate return in power and glory. He knows his future and who his hope is in. Is he still alive, or have his enemies succeeded in killing him? I do not know, but since his first day as a follower of Jesus, he has been good with either outcome because he knows his ultimate outcome.

The End Times (24:36-51)

If the temple was not going to be around much longer, then it was not a building or any structure that Jesus was concerned about. If Jesus was not concerned about buildings, then that should not be the concern of his followers either. If not the temple or a church building, where does this road of following Jesus lead?

Jesus drew his followers' thoughts to the end times and what will happen then. As you read through the latter part of chapter 24 and chapter 25, there are several thoughts that Jesus mentioned multiple times. If he repeated himself, then it should be something that his followers need to hold on to dearly.

One of Jesus's repeated thoughts was that the end time would be the time of his return (24:39, 42, 44, 50). This was also something Jesus taught in his earlier words (24:27, 30-31). He would leave them, but he will return. The impression made through the teachings was that Jesus' return would not be imminent, but his followers could count on it.

Jesus also repeated that no one knows when he will return, no one except for the Father in heaven (24:36, 42, 44, 50; 25:13). The story of Noah was used to illustrate that fact. The examples of a man being taken and another left, a woman being taken and another left, also underscored this teaching. The parables of the owner of the house and the servant left in charge drove this point home.

A third message that ran through this part of Jesus' teachings focused on his followers—would they be prepared when he does return? The disciples of Jesus needed to do something or live in a certain way to be prepared. Most of the people in Noah's day were unprepared. The owner of the house was an example of being prepared, an example Jesus wanted his followers to learn from. The parable of the servant left in charge portrayed two possible outcomes for that servant: a good one if he was prepared, a terrible one if he was not prepared. This last parable hinted at the parables that would soon follow, which would give directions on how to be prepared.

We need to consider one more component of Jesus' teachings. He spoke about judgment. There will be some saved and some judged when Jesus returns. The illustration of the flood had that component of judgment. The illustrations of the man and woman taken, and the man and woman left behind, also had a judgment component. We can see judgment involved with the servant left in charge; he would be rewarded or punished depending on how he carried out his duties. This component of judgment made clear to those twelve men that how they followed Jesus had some bearing on how they would perceive his return, either with joy and anticipation or with fear and dread.

We can find a lot to think over from this section of teaching. Like the earlier blocks, there is much that will challenge us. Perhaps it is good to remember at this point who is the power. It is Jesus, because that is the role that the Father gave him. That is a comforting thought, in one sense, because we can lean on that when the powers of our culture oppress and persecute us. We know that these powers will not have the final say. If we stand firm with Jesus to our end, whatever it may be, then we will be just fine.

However, the thought that Jesus is the power is also challenging to us. Why? Because we are prone to want to be the power ourselves. We want to make the terms for how it all ends for us. Whether we are preachers, church members, or just wear the name Christian, we tend to want our preparations for Jesus' return to be good enough. If we look around, we can see a lot of preparation that sure looks different, and everybody thinks Jesus will be fine with that because he will surely accept whatever we have done. Some believe being a member of some church, having their name on the roll, is enough preparation. Some believe just being a regular attendee at a church worship service is enough. Then there are those who think just an occasional appearance at a worship service is enough preparation. There are those who take any connection with a church out of the preparation altogether. They believe just being a good person who does more good than bad is enough. You can even meet people who think it all boils down to whether or not they view themselves as a believer in Jesus—how they live doesn't even matter. People are all over the place when it comes to preparation to get to heaven.

If you are thinking anywhere along those lines, you will be challenged by Jesus being the power. He will be hard for you to hear and follow when he is calling you to do something you do not want to do or to be someone you do not want to be. Are you willing to acknowledge someone is over you and follow his ways over your ways?

Allow me to share another troubling experience. I have witnessed many Christians come out of Bible study sessions, having learned something new that they were not comfortable with. Did they follow Jesus in those teachings? Too often, I heard disciples state they were not ready to follow that teaching, so they compromised and found a place where they could all be at peace and be comfortable. As I look at these five blocks of teachings from Jesus, I find no place where he compromised and allowed his followers to stop anywhere short of what he had called them to do. What do our actions reveal about who we really acknowledge as the power in the kingdom? Do we follow Jesus's lead, or do we expect him to follow our lead?

Since we are already in, up to our necks, another thought needs to be considered regarding these teachings. There are a lot of people who seem to have a pretty good idea when Jesus is going to return. There are some who have even been brassy enough to proclaim a certain date. We seem to be overly occupied with knowing the when of his return. We would be better served if we just accept what Jesus said: nobody knows either the day or the hour. If we can accept that, then maybe we will focus more on what Jesus wants us to focus on: just be prepared for him to come at any time. If we are prepared, when he comes does not really matter because we will eagerly anticipate it and steadfastly wait for it.

As we draw these teachings down to us, we do not want to fail to draw down the teachings about judgment. Jesus' words will not pass away, for they will be proven true when he returns. There will be people who will be glad when he returns, and there will be people weeping. They will realize then, too late, that they believed in the wrong power. They will realize that they are not prepared, and they will face a judgment that Jesus described as a place where there will be weeping and gnashing of teeth. That is not a pretty picture in anyone's mind. Instead of passing over or ignoring Jesus' teachings on judgment, we need to hear him. This can be motivation for us to prepare so that his judgment will not come upon us.

I live in a culture where sermons focus a lot on love, doing good deeds, encouragement, joy, celebration, etc. Those are all wonderful aspects of the kingdom and of the kingdom message. However, the harder teachings seem to get passed over a lot. Maybe they are briefly mentioned at times, maybe scarcely mentioned, or not even at all. These are the teachings about sin (yes, there is still such a thing as sin), judgment (yes, there is still a day of judgment coming), and about hell (and yes, there is a blazing fire of hell in the future of all who do not follow Jesus). It is as if we believe these things will go away if we do not talk about them or believe in them anymore. Perhaps that would be the case if people were the ultimate power. However, Jesus made clear in this block of teaching that he is that power, and his words will not pass away. They will be proven true. We do ourselves no favor, nor anyone else, when we are silent about Jesus' teachings on judgment.

Like I said, we got into Jesus' teachings pretty deep, right up to our necks. Perhaps you feel as if you are going to choke on them. I would not be surprised if that was the case for the twelve men who first heard these teachings. They did not have much time to reflect on Jesus' teachings because dark days were swiftly upon them. Maybe you need some time to take all this in, and maybe that time is afforded to you. If so, do some praying and reflecting. Ask the Lord for understanding and the courage to accept whatever teaching or insight bears the weight of truth. Remember, Jesus wants you to successfully walk this road. He will help you.

The Three Parables (25:1-46)

As we have read Jesus' fifth block of teaching to his followers, we have seen a clear progression in his teachings. For example, one of the anchors for his followers was the temple mount. When Jesus foretold its destruction, he removed that anchor. What would his followers put their hope in then? Or in whom? Jesus taught them to put their hope in him; he was now their anchor. He was the only power that would be standing at the end of time, so only he could fulfill their hope and be their anchor. However, they would have to learn how to follow and trust him when he was not physically present.

Another example of this progression in Jesus' teachings was his shift from focusing on the existence of the temple to emphasizing his followers' faithfulness. How would they get through all the hard things to come, and how would they prepare for Jesus' return? This shift was crucial for them. This brings us to the focus on the preparation of Jesus' followers. Jesus covered that through the telling of three parables. These parables are interconnected, and each one builds on the previous. Our task now is to understand each parable and see the connection as one leads into the next.

The Ten Virgins (25:1-13)

Jesus started his first parable with a variation of a phrase he had used many times in his teachings to his followers: *"The kingdom of heaven will be like..."* He used a familiar sight to his followers to paint his picture of his kingdom—a wedding procession. I found two sources that helped me understand this procession better; you can find others as well. The two that helped me are: *The Life and Times of Jesus the Messiah* by Alfred Edersheim, MacDonald Publishing Company, Book V, Chapter 7, pp. 453-459; and *Matthew* by Matthew Chouinard, College Press NIV Commentary, 1997, pp. 437-439. You can read through these resources and others if you like.

Culturally, there were certain components of a Jewish wedding that Jesus tapped into with his parable. Before the wedding ceremony, the groom would have met with the bride's father to set the terms for the dowry. Upon agreement, the future husband would then go to build a home for him and his wife-to-be. This often would be an addition to his own father's house. The bride would then wait for her future husband to come get her, not knowing exactly when that time would be. She would ready her possessions so that she could go with her husband when he did arrive.

When the future husband had completed their home, he would send word that he was coming for his bride. Her family would then make preparations to receive him. The bride would make her final preparations. No one knew the exact time of his arrival, but it would be at night. A bridal party would consist of attendants for the bridegroom and the bride. Some of those attendants would be ten maidens, or virgins, who would lead a procession from the bride's home to their new home where the wedding banquet would take place. Since it was at night, they would need lamps to light the way, and oil for their lamps. This is the part of the wedding night that Jesus used for his parable.

In the parable, Jesus is the bridegroom, and his followers are the ten virgins. They could be the wise ones or the foolish ones, depending on their preparations. Since no one knew when the bridegroom would actually arrive, it was wise for those virgin attendants to have extra oil with them. In the parable, five were wise enough to do that, but five were foolish and did not have any extra oil with them. They all fell asleep as they waited for the bridegroom's arrival. When he finally did arrive, only then did the foolish virgins realize they did not have enough oil to lead the wedding procession. They were not adequately prepared. As a result, they had to hurry off to buy some more oil, and they were not present when the bridegroom did arrive. The five other virgins were prepared and fulfilled their role as they led the procession to the new home and the wedding banquet. Because they had adequately prepared, they were able to go into the banquet. The five foolish virgins arrived later and were shut out. Even when they pleaded for entry, the bridegroom denied them. They missed the banquet because they were not adequately prepared.

What impression did this parable have on those twelve men? Jesus' prior teachings about Noah, the people taken and left, the owner of the house, and the servant left in charge underscored that Jesus' followers needed to be alert and ready for Jesus' return because no one knew when it would be. This parable introduced a new thought to the twelve about how to be alert and ready: make adequate preparations. If such preparations were not made, they would miss out on the banquet, the parable's image for the kingdom.

The parable ends with a phrase Jesus had spoken multiple times since starting this last half of his teaching: *"Therefore keep watch, because you do not know the day or the hour."* This ties Jesus' teaching about personal preparation with how one is ready for his return. His followers were not to keep watch by just sitting around anticipating Jesus would show up someday. Instead, they were to keep watch by using every day for preparations, by engaging in what he had given them to do.

Thus, this parable lays the groundwork for the next parable by drawing the followers' focus to their need to make personal preparations for Jesus' return at the end of time. If they were to go through the loss of the temple, through personal persecution and death, only the return of Jesus offered them the hope that made such sacrifices worthwhile. However, each follower just heard that their hope would be pointless if they were not prepared. No doubt those followers were listening intently as Jesus proceeded to give them more information about those preparations.

When you take the time to reflect on this parable, and please do, be sure to understand what Jesus wants you to know about how you need to prepare for his return. This is a personal responsibility. No follower of Jesus can rely on what someone else has done; we each bear responsibility to make sure we are prepared. We can encourage one another, and we each need to be encouraged; however, at some point, each disciple is called to step up and live into their calling and mission.

You may struggle with these parables if you understand that your salvation depends solely on your faith and God's grace. These parables add another necessary element: your preparations. Your actions as a follower of Jesus impact what will happen to you when Jesus returns.

Listen to Jesus in these parables; he is the power that will be standing at the end time, so he is the one you need to hear. As Jesus said earlier, *let those who have ears hear.*

Ask yourself: *What activity fills my day, my life?* Does it contribute to my preparation for Jesus' return? Maybe not every activity of your day does, and maybe it doesn't have to. But does any of it? How you go through your days and through your life matters. Those activities are what fill your days and your life. They matter in a huge way to followers of Jesus because they are your preparations for his return.

The Bags of Gold (25:14-30)

Some older translations refer to this parable as the Parable of the Talents. That would be an accurate literal translation of Jesus' original words. However, many cultures view talents as abilities and not as money; the latter was the meaning of the word when Jesus spoke this parable. So referring to the parable as bags of gold is true to the intended meaning of Jesus' words. If you were wondering why this difference in wording exists, that is the reason.

Jesus paints another image in this parable that develops the idea and need for preparation on each follower's part. In this parable, Jesus is portrayed by the man going on a journey, the master. His disciples are represented by one of the three men entrusted with their master's gold. Again, which man is representative of a particular follower depends on what each disciple does with the *gold* given to him or her.

The parable relates how three different servants were given differing amounts of gold, each according to his ability. What these men did with the gold determined what happened to each one. Two men put the gold to work and doubled what was given to them. They were welcomed and rewarded when the day of settling accounts arrived. The third man was different. He chose to mistrust the master, and he did nothing with what he was given other than hide it in a hole. When he brought back that amount, having done nothing with it, his master was not pleased and cast him out into the darkness. What happened to him was reminiscent of what happened to the servant left in charge of other servants, who chose to do evil and ultimately was not prepared for his master's return. The servants in both parables were thrown into a place where there would be weeping and gnashing of teeth.

What did those twelve men hear when they heard this parable? Jesus would give each of them something that he would expect them to use for his purposes, to bring about a harvest for him. Maybe these *bags of gold* represented opportunities and responsibilities, some kind of work to be done. Maybe they represented something more. We will see. What is important to see at this point is that Jesus would not give each follower the same work, for they were all different. Each had different abilities, different strengths and weaknesses. He would give each follower a work that each was capable of doing, and could do well.

They also heard that if they lived up to Jesus' expectations, a harvest would result, and they would be received with joy and rewarded. They also heard that if anyone decided not to do the work given him, nothing positive would happen, and they would be rejected, judged, and cast out from Jesus' presence on his return. They would be cast into a terrible place of judgment. The obvious question for those twelve followers would center on what Jesus would give them to do.

The question those followers would have had as they listened to Jesus might mirror your own question. Have you ever wondered what Jesus expects of you? Have you ever found yourself comparing yourself to other followers and getting discouraged because you did not have the same abilities they have, the same strengths? As your thoughts are being drawn to your preparations, perhaps you are wondering if you will hear these words from Jesus on that day: *"Well done, good and faithful servant! You have been faithful with a few things. I will put you in charge of many things. Come and share your master's happiness!"* Or maybe you fear you will hear these words from him: *"Throw that worthless servant outside, into the darkness, where there will be weeping and gnashing of teeth."*

If you are experiencing one of these two feelings, you are where Jesus wants you to be as you listen to him. He wants you to realize that there is a lot at stake here. Your response to what he gives you matters greatly…for you. The next parable can give you peace as you receive the final piece of guidance you need. Or it will elevate your fear if you find Jesus calling you into something you will refuse to do. Let this thought give you comfort as we head into the last parable: Jesus gives you something to do that he knows you can do; he gives to each according to his or her ability. Jesus knows you and believes in what you can do.

The Sheep and the Goats (25:31-46)

How does Jesus call his followers to prepare for his return? What are the works he will put before them? In this last parable, Jesus gave some very concrete examples. Read the parable again. What are your initial thoughts? What are your initial feelings? Did you expect this list of examples?

The parable began with Jesus coming and sitting on his throne. Those twelve had heard that theme throughout these teachings. They had heard it was necessary for them to stay faithful and endure, putting their hope in Jesus. They had heard they needed to be ready and to prepare. In this parable, they heard the specifics that would help them understand what was truly important to their leader.

Jesus told them he would come with his angels and sit on his throne, and he told them about the judgment that would take place. All people who had ever lived would be brought before him in the parable. He would separate them and determine their eternity. His followers would be in that large crowd of humanity as well, mixed among the people who were not followers. Then the separation would take place, like a shepherd separating his sheep from his goats. Followers of Jesus might find themselves as one of the sheep, or possibly as one of the goats.

In the parable, being a sheep was good; being a goat was bad. The sheep would be welcomed into eternal life, into the kingdom the Father had prepared for them. The goats would find themselves condemned and thrown into an eternal fire.

What was the determining factor by which people would be judged in the parable? Jesus said it would be how they treated the least among them. Jesus saw those people as his brothers and sisters. Would those who claimed to follow him see them in the same way? Their lives as his followers, their mission as his followers, would be filled with opportunities to show how they regarded the least among them. How his followers treated them and met them in their pain would be known by Jesus, their King.

Jesus gave six examples of people who would be seen as the least among them: the hungry, the thirsty, the stranger, the naked, the sick, the prisoner. It was not an exhaustive list; there were many others whom Jesus could have mentioned, but parables were not intended to be exhaustive. Yet, these six examples would suffice in challenging those twelve men.

These twelve men were not rich, at least not anymore. They had given up everything to follow Jesus. There were women who financially supported them and Jesus, which was a major shift for those men. Even before Jesus showed up, they would have known hunger, and they would know it again. How would they respond then to another person in need of food, if they were hungry themselves? Whose need would they find it imperative to meet?

Those twelve followers had come across many strangers and would meet many more. They lived in a culture where hospitality was inherent in their identity. Would they offer hospitality to a stranger? What about a stranger from another country who did not speak their language or share their beliefs? Would they give up a bed in their own home for that person?

Those original followers knew there were people in prison. Perhaps they knew people in prison. However, it was not typically good to be a known associate with someone in prison. That could bring the person who knew the prisoner under suspicion, observation, and maybe into prison themselves. Would those twelve risk their freedom to go and take care of a person in prison?

Would they give clothes to a person in need if the only clothes they had were the ones they were wearing? Would they go to a well and draw water to give a thirsty person a drink? Would they risk personal sickness by caring for someone who was sick?

In that culture, Jesus found six examples to test his followers. Would they care for the least among them—people most would ignore, or stay away from, or not even notice? It was one thing to proclaim to Jesus they would follow him when Jesus was with them. It was one thing to do what Jesus told them to do when he was standing right next to them. Would they do the same things when he wasn't looking over their shoulders?

They had recently heard Jesus' teachings about honoring people that their culture deemed unworthy of such honor. It did not take them long to come up short in following those teachings then. What would they do in the future? Would they rise to the occasion, opportunity, and responsibility? Or would they come up short again? Would Jesus' teachings sink in and become not their second nature, but their first nature? It had to, because that would determine whether or not they would be welcomed into eternal life. Were they sheep or goats? It all came down to whether they would put into practice what they would be telling others to do. He had condemned the teachers of the law and the Pharisees for preaching a message but not practicing it themselves. Jesus would not accept the same low standard from his followers.

These final three parables built on one another to point the original twelve followers of Jesus from focusing on a building to focusing on something else. The first parable called them to each prepare for his return. The second parable instructed them to work with whatever bags of gold he gave them. The third parable revealed those bags of gold were the least among them that they would encounter, and their preparation was how they treated each of those people. That is where Jesus wanted his followers' focus to be.

Those twelve men had asked Jesus what they may have thought was a simple question. What they received in this last block of teaching was literally a "come to Jesus" talk. Time was running out for Jesus to walk physically with them. They had some hard and terrible times coming their way, so Jesus gave them some final preparation. They would soon have to show through their actions if they really were his followers. How they would treat the least of those that came their way was something Jesus would watch very closely. He wanted to know who really followed him and who was just talking.

As you consider what Jesus taught in this last parable regarding the preparation he was looking for, you might be thinking that Jesus had made a shift from emphasizing preaching to doing good works. So you might think Jesus is letting you off the hook from proclaiming his message about the kingdom. If that is where your thoughts are taking you, let me help reel you back in line with Jesus.

Jesus never minimized the need for his followers to care about others and help them in their times of need. Go back and look at his teachings. The fulfillment of the law was doing to others as his followers would want others to do to them. Giving financially to the poor was important. Not judging others, honoring those others overlooked, and using the power Jesus had given them to help those that others avoided were part and parcel of Jesus' teachings. When asked what the greatest command was, Jesus answered and also added a second command about loving others. Jesus never diminished loving the least. Nor does his focus on them in this last teaching diminish his call for his followers to proclaim his teachings to others. The message was key to Jesus' mission from the very start, and so it must be for all who follow him. We need to hear Jesus calling us to both; that is our road.

Let's pick up again on the least among us. Who are they? We can be just as selective as those twelve men if we are not listening to Jesus. Perhaps in my culture, the white follower of Jesus fails to see the black follower of Jesus as important, and therefore, fails to help him or her in their time of need. Perhaps the black follower of Jesus fails to see the Hispanic follower and help him or her in their time of need. Perhaps the Hispanic follower is focused solely on his own people and does not see the Asian follower… Perhaps the follower who is a citizen of one country feels no obligation to help the follower from another country. Perhaps the least among us is a child, an undocumented immigrant, or a group of strangers tucked away in a dementia facility across town. We are surrounded by the least among us, yet they can be invisible to us if we do not see them as Jesus does.

Recently in my life, I met an activity director for an adult assisted living facility. The residents in her facility had Alzheimer's. The people were grouped in three different levels of care, levels that were determined by how far the disease had advanced. The director told me a heartbreaking tale. Many of these residents had lived their lives connected to some church. They loved to worship God, but now they were not able to go to those churches and worship with other believers. Then she told me how she had tried for over a year to get people from churches to come to that facility and conduct worship services for the residents. What did she have to show for all her effort? Nothing. No one accepted the invitation. No Christians had come. Then the director said something that became seared on my heart, *"Alzheimer's shouldn't have the power to rob people of the opportunity to worship God."* It became clear to me that I was being introduced to some of the least of these brothers and sisters of Jesus. I had a decision to make. If you had been in my place, what would your decision have been? I made mine. Will your decision lead you to seek out some of those *least of these?*

We gather in church buildings on Sundays, in fancy and beautiful buildings, wearing nice clothes, preaching and listening to messages that sound a lot like what Jesus taught. Yet what do we do with the *bags of gold* he continually entrusts us with? Those bags of gold in the second parable turned out to be more than just opportunities and responsibilities. They turned out to be people, the least among us. Do we have ears to hear Jesus speak to us? I hope so. We need to hear him. There are people now, all around us, who need us to be hearing Jesus. We also have an eternity that is going to be impacted by whether we hear him clearly enough that we will follow him regarding the bags of gold given to each of us.

I step back a moment and step into a relevant thought with you that is needed now. As we open our eyes, ears, and hearts to the least among us, we need to make sure that we do not hear Jesus saying something that he was not saying. There are cultures that would have us embrace some people as being the least among us. They will claim these people are hated and treated as less than others. It will look that way on the surface. However, a closer look will reveal that culture is pressuring followers of Jesus to accept and embrace people who have rejected God's righteousness. Jesus loved all people and died for all people, but he never accepted the rejection of the call to righteousness. Rejection of God's righteousness does not make a person one of the least of these; it makes them a person who is in danger of receiving Jesus' judgment. Followers of Jesus have to discern how to respond in love, not hatred, but still call these precious people to God's righteousness. Followers of Jesus cannot jettison any of Jesus' teachings to accommodate people who choose sin over righteousness. Disciples of Jesus need to hear all of his teachings and let him, not culture, guide them on how to love those walking a different road from Jesus.

As you reflect on what you have read in this final block of teaching, I offer you some questions that can guide your reflections. Who or what is the power you put your hope in? Are there any anchors in your life that get in the way of Jesus being your anchor? If there are, do they need to be removed? Do you stand firm with Jesus when your life gets hard? Will you stay on the road of following Jesus, no matter how hard it gets? Are there any people who are the least of these that you have failed to see? If so, what do you need to do so that you will see them and be able to respond to them? Are you making adequate preparations for when Jesus returns?

Seat Belt Check

Why do heroic lives inspire us, spurring us on to be better people than we are? Have you ever wondered? We know many people who live comfortable lives that do not require great sacrifices of them. We may be drawn to that, but those stories do not inspire us. We know of people who live luxuriously and have so many wonderful things that we can easily become envious. Yet, those lives do not inspire us either. However, when we hear about or watch someone go through terrible times, persevering and overcoming against all odds, we are inspired. We long to be like them. Why is that? We notice someone living heroically, and we are inspired by heroes. When I consider such things, I understand the power of the example that heroic lives have. So I offer that to you as your seat belt check, just in case you are thinking about bailing on Jesus after this final block of teachings.

First, if you are about to bail, decide for the moment that you will stand firm. Then look around and find a follower of Jesus who is standing firm. That is the hero you need at this time. Meet with that follower and ask them to share how and why they stand firm with Jesus. Ask them to tell you their story of how sticking with Jesus has cost them. Let them tell you whatever is on their heart that can encourage you. Through this conversation, that follower will become one of your heroes, and they will inspire you to rise up and meet your challenge so that you can live heroically and stand firm with Jesus as well. Meet with them as often as you can.

Second, you can actually strap on an additional seat belt that will help you stand firm. Look around you and find a follower who seems to be close to bailing on Jesus. Humbly approach that person and ask to meet with them one-on-one. When you meet, let them know that you see them; tell them how important they are to you. Then share with them a time when you almost bailed because of the adversity you were facing. Let them know the blessings that came because you stuck with Jesus. Then allow them to share with you whatever they need to. They might tell you about their adversity, their discouragement, and their struggles to stand firm. You might find that their eyes will watch you afterward because they see you now as their hero. You were struggling, but you are still standing, and you cared enough to see them and reach out. You were actually living heroically at that point.

We are surrounded by heroes of faith, and each of us can be a hero of faith. There are enough seat belts to go around for all. May none of us bail when following Jesus gets hard.

Have You Decided to Follow Jesus?

We have walked through the five blocks of teaching where Jesus focused on what He expected from those who chose to follow Him. We have taken a *Jesus look* at the road He has called us to walk. Of course, this look was just based on five teachings that Matthew recorded, and there are definitely other places in Matthew's gospel where Jesus taught His followers more. When Jesus responded to a teacher of the law, in Matthew 22:34-40, regarding the greatest command, no doubt His followers learned a lesson they needed to hear.

Understanding how to follow Jesus requires understanding the other gospels as well. When John wrote in his gospel the teachings of Jesus regarding the good shepherd and the sheep in John 10, those teachings are also important for followers of Jesus. Luke helps us listen to Jesus through the eyes of someone who came later. He includes teachings not found in the other gospels. Mark helps us understand Jesus' teachings in the heat of conflict between the kingdom of Jesus and the kingdom of the devil. We learn from all of these.

Our purpose is not to discount or minimize the teachings of Jesus outside of these five sections of Matthew's gospel. Our efforts are intended to shine a light on teachings that may not have been understood as they should have been, both in their meaning and importance. Matthew was the only writer to record the Great Commission where Jesus instructed His disciples to make disciples by baptizing them and teaching them what He had taught. Only Matthew has these teachings from Jesus to His followers in five blocks. Matthew provides us with an important format to hear and know these teachings.

Did you notice that when we looked at these blocks of teaching, Jesus did not teach anything about the importance of attending church services? This is not to say that is unimportant, but that it did not make Jesus' top five teachings. Did you notice He did not teach anything about tithing or offerings? Again, this does not make those practices unnecessary; obviously, those teachings are elsewhere in Holy Scripture. However, Jesus had other matters He felt it was important to teach.

Did you notice in these teachings, He spoke more about danger and crosses than He did about being safe? Did you notice that His teachings made you feel more uncomfortable than comfortable? He spoke more about what His followers should give than what they would get. Did you notice that not only were Jesus' teachings counter-culture to our societies, but they were also counter-cultural to many church cultures?

Like any religion, Christianity can fall into the trap of making really good disciples of a church or of a preacher but not very good disciples of Jesus. Human nature paired with the enemy, Satan, makes that fairly simple and common. This makes us weaker, not stronger. It not only puts us on a different road than Jesus, but it can also put us on a road where we go counter-kingdom culture on Jesus. That is a really dangerous road to be on.

In my time and culture, I noticed how the events of 2020 exposed the weaknesses of many who claim to follow Jesus. We were hit with the pandemic of the Covid virus. It was a new disease that we were all learning about, and because of the news of many people dying, it was a virus that we greatly feared. Government authorities promoted and pushed many policies that were counter-culture to the kingdom and to Jesus' teachings. We isolated; we even stopped meeting for times of worship. We stopped seeking the lost. Going out to do good works and proclaiming the message came to a stop in many places. We did this out of obedience to government authorities, out of concern for others, and out of fear. None of us know how our Teacher will judge or evaluate our response to this virus, but as we reflect and learn from our past, would we say we were listening to Jesus as we went through the pandemic? Specifically, on our present journey, would we have responded differently if we had spent time listening to Jesus in these five blocks of teaching?

In my culture, we were also hit with social unrest because of racial injustice. It was like a double hit that exposed churches in our culture. Our normal way of working through problems as a church had been shut down by Covid, so when the incidents of racial injustice exploded in our culture and piled on top of the pandemic, we struggled with how to respond. Even in churches, there was anger that was spilling out. Disciples who had been in harmony and one in spirit struggled to work across racial identities with the emotions that were pouring out. Some disciples were angry, others fearful. Few knew what to say or how to work through what needed to be worked through. There were those who had been known as followers of Jesus who were taking their cues from social media, from the internet, and other sources in our culture instead of from Jesus. Would we have responded differently to the racial unrest if we had spent time in these five blocks of teaching?

When we look back, we may determine that we did not respond very well to the events of 2020. That would be a pretty fair assessment, but our failures should not surprise us. Satan dropped a whole lot on us in a short period of time. However, will we be able to see that some of our failures, maybe all of them, could have been avoided if we were rooted in these five blocks of teachings from Jesus? We were unprepared for what came at us, and our weaknesses were exposed by the devil. Have we realized that? If we do not, we will fail once more when the devil unloads on us again.

How did eleven of Jesus' first followers end up being such exceptional followers? They sure did not start out that way. They had to learn to seek out Jesus and listen to Him if they were going to hear Him. They grew into being followers of Jesus. Perhaps we experience initial failure when we do not realize our need to continually grow as followers. Perhaps we have grown comfortable with just being church members in good standing because we can do that without the need to keep growing. We can excel at being a pillar of the church that does nothing more than refuse to budge from the same spot. That is a far cry from walking the same road Jesus walked.

It is so easy to assume we are following Jesus when we are actually on a different road. All the voices that are important to us—in our families and churches, friends and associates—may be praising us. Then someone comes along who is actually teaching us what Jesus taught, and we throw up our defenses and shut our ears. This may sound like we are in some unsolvable dilemma, but that could not be further from the truth. Jesus is not hard to understand. We just have to spend time with Him. Matthew has given us a way to do just that.

Did you notice as you went through these five blocks of teaching anything that sounded different from what you have been hearing from others? It wasn't that hard to recognize those teachings, was it? Your struggles come with choosing to hear Jesus or stick with the other voices. We like fitting into our culture and the comforts that affords. That is an easier road to walk. Perhaps one of our first warning lights that flashes in our minds should be when we have an undisturbed sense of comfort in our culture, even in our church culture.

I remember a time when I was firmly entrenched in my comfort with my culture. I was rock solid in line with how my culture responded to people I regarded as illegal aliens. I knew what I believed and knew it was correct. Then I heard a sister pray for a group of illegal aliens who had suffocated in an abandoned truck left in the Arizona heat. She wept as she prayed. Jesus used that follower to disturb my comfort. That led me into a year-long search in the Bible for understanding. It also led me to a couple of nuns who disturbed my comfort even more. These two nuns were being God's touch to help undocumented immigrants in detention and to help their families at times of deportation. That led me on a years-long journey of meeting undocumented immigrants, as I now see them. I knew I could never be comfortable again with my culture's view of these *least of these* that are now in my life. Jesus had brought me to a place where I could, and where I did, hear Him.

In just this one part of my travels down this road of following Jesus, I have discovered that Jesus knows how to shake us up and get our attention when we get detoured from following Him. He knows who to use and what to do to disturb our comfort. He knows how to get His voice in our ears. When He does that to you, you will have to decide if you have ears to hear.

There are so many places in our lives and in our practice of our religion where we can get comfortable. Let's be honest with each other— we all like comfort. We all like being liked. As much as we profess to be individuals, we prefer to run with the pack most of the time. That means most of the people we know will not choose to walk the road that Jesus walked. Yet, if we do not break from the culture that has greatly shaped us, we cannot walk that same road as Jesus, which means we are not following Him. To follow Jesus is to always be in the minority in any culture of this world.

Can any of us successfully follow Jesus down this road? Sure. This is a road anybody can walk if they choose it. Nobody but Jesus walks it perfectly; thankfully, He is there to help us. Every follower grows up as we walk this road, as long as we stay on it. Jesus allows us that, and He helps us grow, just like He did with His first followers. In Jesus, we have a guide, a helper, and a companion on the road. No matter how hard, painful, or scary the road gets, He is there. He is especially there at those places on the road. He sticks with us, and we stick with Him. That is the way the road is successfully traveled.

Following Jesus comes down to a choice between two roads. You now know more about one of those roads because of the teachings of Jesus that Matthew recorded. Commit them to your heart and mind. They are straight from Jesus, and these teachings have not passed away. You will need them as you follow Jesus down this hard road. His words will ultimately be the seat belt that keeps you from bailing.

One of the spiritual songs of my childhood was *"I Have Decided to Follow Jesus."* There were some big statements in that song a child could not fully understand, but they helped shape me in my early years: "the cross before me, the world behind me"; "though none go with me, still I will follow"; "no turning back, no turning back." This song powerfully conveys the decision we all have to make. Will you follow Jesus?

A Final Word

You have in your hands a simple book that, at best, can only poorly convey the teachings of Jesus to all who would follow him. There has never been another teacher like Jesus. This book, like other efforts by followers, serves as a reminder of who we need to listen to if we are going to follow him. Please receive it as such. I hope it helps you hear Jesus.

I also hope you will never be discouraged when you see another follower fail in following Jesus or even abandon him. I hope you will never give up when you witness most of a church following culture instead of Jesus. These things happen too often, and they can discourage us, but they only reinforce how important it is that we have eyes and ears for Jesus above all others.

Believe that you can walk this road successfully—not perfectly, but successfully. Give grace and encouragement to those you meet who are struggling, and receive grace and encouragement from others, especially from Jesus, when you are struggling. Stand firm with Jesus to the end of your road. Jesus will help you succeed.

As you proclaim the message Jesus has given all of his followers, his teachings, do not ever be ashamed or apologetic for the hard teachings they must hear from you. Jesus' teachings will take root in the hearts that hear him and produce a harvest that no person could foresee. Those who have ears to hear Jesus will not be put off by his hard teachings; instead, they will rise to the challenge.

I have shared with you these five blocks of Jesus' teachings in Matthew's gospel. I wish I could tell you I understood their importance a lot earlier than I did. I believe that you do not have to fail where I did. Pass along what you have learned. If you have learned anything through me in this book, you did not hear me—you heard Jesus. Matthew passed these teachings along to his readers, of which I am just one. I am passing the teachings on to you. May you be blessed for passing them on to other followers.

Ke Russo

Start a Ripple…Pray a Wave

The world we live in is broken. We see all around us the power and influence of the devil. You see this and feel it. The good news is that the Good News is the cure for a downward-spiraling culture and a broken world. Imagine a wave for the kingdom sweeping everywhere, bringing spiritual revival. Prayerfully, God will bring such a wave in our times. Perhaps God uses any ripples that his people start to bring about such a wave. Visit **www.StartaripplePrayforawave.com** to explore this opportunity.

Believe that God will work through you and whatever ripples you start. If you want to use this book as a tool to start any number of ripples, here are some ideas:

- Consider the people you are connected to who need to hear these teachings of Jesus so that they can follow him. Get them a book and talk about how you can encourage each other to walk the road Jesus calls you to walk.

- If you are connected to a church, talk with the leaders about having classes or studies that will take disciples through these teachings.

- Reach out to your contacts on social media and encourage them to get a book and read about these teachings of Jesus. Share with them any truths that have impacted you.

- Encourage others to check out the website for more information.

- Ask the Spirit of God to show you where and how to start other ripples.

- Pray for ripples to start everywhere and for those ripples to become a wave.

You are called to be a light so that people can see God through you. You can use this book and other tools on this website to be that light. The kingdom of heaven is not limited by the reach of a book or a website, however, you might determine that these tools can be used to help the kingdom spread. Followers of Jesus do not have to accept the brokenness of the world or the downward spiral of society. We have the power of God to draw from. If God has used me to help you fully step into your calling as a follower of Jesus, then it is an honor to partner with you.

May God bless every ripple and send a wave!

www.StartaripplePrayforawave.com